AF552849

Contemporary Issues in BUSINESS FINANCE

Contemporary Issues in BUSINESS FINANCE

Editor

OMPRAKASH KAJIPET

Associate Professor of Commerce

Kakatiya University

KARIMNAGAR

DISCOVERY PUBLISHING HOUSE

NEW DELHI—110 002

First Published–2000

Reprinted-2011

ISBN 81-7141-561-X

Published by

DISCOVERY PUBLISHING HOUSE
4831/24, Ansari Road, Prahlad Street,
Darya Ganj, New Delhi-110002 (India)
Phone: 3279245 • Fax: 91-11-3253475
E-mail:dph@indiatimes.com

PRINTED IN INDIA

Printed at Mehra Offset Press, Delhi.

Foreword

Business Finance has emerged as one of the critical areas of corporate management in recent years. It is an area, which has been undergoing tremendous and very fast changes both in philosophy and practice. This is mainly because of ongoing process of economic liberalisation and globalisation in the country. The process of economic restructuring at the government-level and the entry of multinational corporate bodies at the industry-level forced the Indian corporate bodies to think, plan, and act in an innovative manner in managing the scarce financial resources placed at their command in the most efficient manner. In doing so, the managers of the Indian companies should invariably should keep themselves update with the intricacies and implications of the different contemporary developments in the field of finance. I hope this edited volume will serve towards this end.

The contemporary issues like buy-back of shares, exchange risk management, depository services, rationalisation of tax laws, management of regional financial institutions, foreign capital flows, and security markets in post-reforms era were dealt with in this volume. I strongly believe that the scholarly contributions from experienced academicians on these issues will be an invaluable addition to the existing literature available on the subject. The book is believed to fill in the gaps in the information needs relating to the contemporary developments in the area of finance.

My student, Dr. Omprakash has made a commendable effort in collecting the scholarly contributions from eminent and experienced academicians on vital issues of business finance. I appreciate his idea of bringing out this edited volume consisting some of the best papers presented in the proceedings of 52nd annual conference of Indian Commerce Association held at L.N. Mithila University, Dharbhanga, Bihar, which may otherwise go unnoticed by the interested readers. I hope this volume is useful to finance professionals, academicians, researchers and students.

PROF. K. RAJESHWAR RAO
Dept. of Commerce &
Business Management
Kakatiya University,
Warangal—506 009 (A.P.).

Acknowledgements

At the outset I acknowledge with a deep sense of gratitude and appreciation, all the great encouragement, and guidance received from all my teachers—Prof. A. Shankaraiah, Prof. K. Rajeshwar Rao, Prof. G. Krishnamurthy, and Prof. G.V. Bhavani Prasad of Department of Commerce and Business Management, Kakatiya University, Warangal from time to time throughout my career as teacher. I am also indebted to Prof. V. Surendar, Prof. D. Obul Reddy, and Prof. H. Venkateshwarlu of Department of Commerce, Osmania University, Hyderabad, who infact suggested me the idea of bringing out this edited volume incorporating some of the best papers presented in technical session on "Emerging Issues in Business Finance" at 50th annual conference of Indian Commerce Association held at L.N. Mithila University, Dharbhanga, Bihar.

I will be failing in my duty if I do not express my deep sense of gratitude and appreciation to all the contributors, who have graciously responded to my request and permitted me to include their scholarly contributions in this volume.

I am also grateful to my colleagues—Prof. O. Ghanshyam Das, Prof. T. Joga Chary, Dr. P. Krishnama Chary, Dr. Shaik Ahmed Hussain, and Shri T. Bharath and friends—Sri V. Rana Pratap, and Dr. D. Himachalam of S.V. University, Tirupati, who constantly encouraged and motivated me to complete this academic endeavour successfully.

I am also grateful to my wife, Mrs. Surekha, and my daughters Prashanti and Prathyusha, who have co-operated with me during my preoccupation with the work of this book by sacrificing some of their pleasure-sharing moments with me.

Last but not the least, I would be happy to place on record my profound gratitude and appreciation to Sri. Tilak Wasan and his team of Discovery Publishing House, New Delhi, the publishers of this Book, who readily agreed to take up the task of bringing out this edited volume in a short-span of time in the present shape.

February 29, 2000 *Omprakash Kajipet*
Karimnagar

Contents

Efficient Market Hypothesis and the Securities Market in India in the Post-Reform Era

Dr. Pranab Kumar Bhattacharyya*

The structure of the securities market can be viewed in terms of relationship between the different groups of individuals and institutions who constitute the market. Securities investment business is all about market risks and the risk taking abilities of the market participants. The major socio-economic role of the securities market is the valuing of securities and the provision of a well-run market place where investors can buy and sell securities. The proper valuation of securities is important as it provides signals for the allocation of scarce capital resources. This implies a particular structure in which no constituent group or subgroup can have any significant power advantage over the others and therefore can be in no position to influence the performance of the market in any way. "The main effect of efficiency should be that it precludes most, if not all, investors from being able systematically to out perform the market"[1].

"In order that the share prices are correctly valued and that the share exchange mechanism is well run, we need a perfect market, the major requirements of which are:

a) homogeneity of the goods;
b) many buyers and sellers;
c) freedom of entry and exit;
d) unlimited supplies of stocks and shares; and
e) perfect knowledge".[2]

* Professor, Department of Commerce, University of Kalyani, Kalyani, West Bengal.

The securities markets of the developed countries have generally met the first four requirements, in so far as they impose no serious constraints on the functioning of exchange mechanism. The fifth condition, perfect knowledge, requires that all knowledge relating to the value of a company is known and that this knowledge is accurately conveyed in share prices. It also means that the market prices of securities reflect all available information and, therefore, higher return over and above what the market can offer is not possible. Viewed from this angle, one can derive the fact that the efficiency of the securities market is characterised not with the exclusion of risk but with the accuracy in the calculation of risks incorporated. "The essence of a correct price is not that it predicts the future but that it fully captures the uncertainties of the future".[3]

On the basis of the extent of assimilation of information the efficiency of securities market can be studied under three heads; weak efficiency, semi-strong efficiency and strong efficiency.[4] The market is efficient in the weak sense if share prices fully reflect the information implied by all price movements. Future price movement, in effect, are totally independent of previous movements implying the absence of any definite rate of return in future. The market is efficient in the semi-strong sense if share prices respond instantaneously and without bias to newly published information whether or not the users of information might differ amongst themselves about the significance of new data. The implication is that the prices that are actually arrived at in such a market would invariably represent the best interpretation of the information. The market is efficient in the strong sense if share prices reflect not only published information but all relevant information including data not yet publicly available. These three levels are not independent of one another. The market which is efficient in the semi-strong sense is also efficient in the weak sense and the market which is efficient in the strong sense is also efficient in the semi-strong and weak sense.

For proper identification of market imperfections or the level of efficiency, the capital market may be viewed as one consisting of three different segments: (1) the Capital Allocation Market, that is, primary market where funds from savers are distributed amongst productive users of capital; (2) the Financial Securities Market, that is secondary market, where the securities owned by the suppliers of capital are traded by them; and (3) the Financial Information Market, where information is transmitted by, amongst others, the productive users of capital to the suppliers.[5]

The standard classification of market efficiency into three levels, in the context of the above division between the securities market and the information market, appeared somewhat misleading. The weak and the semi-strong levels are concerned with the processing of information, whereas the strong level efficiency is concerned with the production of information and therefore relates to the efficiency of the information market. Thus, if the capital market is found to be inefficient in the strong sense, then it follows that this is a criticism of the information market and of corporate financial reporting practices. But as the three segments make a composite whole, the stock market efficiency as a whole depends on the efficiency of each of the three segments separately. Inefficiency in one segment of the market can jeopardise fair valuation of securities and efficient trading even if the other two are efficient.

In the real world, imperfections are there; transaction costs and information costs may lead to non-availability of information to all participants equally and at the same time this may create pockets of better absorption and poor absorption. This may lead to less than or more than equilibrium profits, namely excess profits or losses. Thus, the efficient market hypothesis has been found to have limited existence in the real world. The results have been almost unanimous in supporting the weak or semi-strong form of efficient market hypothesis. In such a situation the Random Walk hypothesis holds good in stock market operations. If, on the other hand, the market is truly efficient then the fundamentalist will be successful only when he has insider information or he has the superior ability of analysing publicly available information and gaining insight into the future of the firm or he uses the above insider information or his superior ability to reach long term buy, sell and hold investment decisions.

In India markets are not efficient, information are not free and easily accessible and the market does not fully absorb immediately all the available information. In this scenario market failures come from any one or more of the following sources.

Free-riding by the investors: Free-riding by the investors refer to a situation where the investors, being incapable of monitoring and analysing information themselves in a systematic manner, depend upon the services provided by the incompetent professionals and institutional investors. As the financial information thus provided does not convey perfect idea about the state of the economy, the industry and the company, the investments made on the basis of such information becomes vulnerable to risks.

Adverse selection of scrips by the investors : The second important source of market failure is the adverse selection of scrips by the investors. Imperfect securities markets are characterised by inadequate and misleading information. Under the situation the investors cannot distinguish between good and bad scrips, and thus the high risk low quality securities offered at comparatively attractive prices become their obvious choice. In the process the good securities offered by good companies elude the investors. But ultimately when their investments fail to give them good returns, the investors lose faith in the market and gradually distance themselves from the market.

Moral hazard problems of investment managers : An imperfect market also paves the way for excessive speculation by the investment managers and security dealers. Sometimes the investment managers, in order to make personal gains, put the investors money in the high-risk scrips while in some cases they do so at the instance of the investors who demand higher returns. But in reality, as the gap between the expected return and the market return widens, the investors start losing interest in the process of investment and finally withdraw themselves from the securities market.

An analysis of the developments in the new issue market in India in the post reform period, as depicted in the Table 1 below, indicates that the amount of new issues, public and rights issues taken together, increased steadily from Rs. 3,955 crore in 1990-91 to Rs. 21, 850 crore in 1993-94 and from 1994-95 the amount of new issues started declining remarkably. It would also appear from the table that, till 1993-94 the size of public issues increased which was also true in case of rights issues. But subsequently the size of issues declined in both the cases. Thus, it can be said that the atmosphere of hope created by the economic reform did not last long.

TABLE–1
Public and Rights Issues 1989-97 (Rs. Crores)

	Public Issues		Rights Issues	
	No. of Issues	Amount	No. of Issues	Amount
1989-90	187	2793.26	N.A.	N.A.
1990-91	141	1704.35	209	2250.66
1991-92	196	1711.36	316	3851.17
1992-93	528	6060.83	488	12629.81
1993-94	770	12544.04	384	9306.22
1994-95	1343	13311.60	351	6793.34
1995-96	1428	11822.18	291	6519.14
1996-97	753	11648.20	131	2724.43

Source : The Prime Directory 1997, New Delhi, p. 0-15.

Another disturbing feature that has come to surface is that, the finance sector mainly the Non-Banking Finance Companies have, of late, emerged as the dominant player in the new issue market. "Like the previous year, fiscal 1996-97 also continued to be dominated by the finance sector. As many as 264 issues (35 per cent) in the year were from this sector, who together offered Rs. 7,895 crore, cornering 68 per cent of the total amount. In 1995-96, 49 companies had been from this sector raising 53 per cent of that years amount".[6] This clearly confirms the declining role of the manufacturing sector in the capital market and also the desire of the investors to make quick profits. During the same period the response from the public to the new issues also declined on all counts. For example, in cases of as many as 330 issues or in 44 per cent of the total issues in 1996-97 the last dates of subscription had to be extended to the last closing dates. The corresponding figures for 1995-96 were 217 issues or 15 per cent for 1994-95, 45 issues or 3 per cent and for 1993-94, 136 issues or 18 per cent respectively.[7] Similarly, over the years from 1993-94 to 1996-97, response to the rights issues also declined continuously. In 1996-97 the issue dates of 37 right issues, forming 28 per cent of such issues, had to be extended. The corresponding figures for 1995-96, 1994-95 and 1993-94 were 25 per cent, 11 per cent and 18 per cent respectively.[8] The depressed market condition is confirmed further by steady decline in equity issues at premium during the period 1994-95 to 1996-97. In 1996-97, the premium issues comprised a meagre 21 per cent of the total mobilisation in comparison to 46 per cent in 1994-95 and 43 per cent in 1995-96.[9] Lastly, in the depressed market the existing companies continued to dominate in terms of new issues. All this clearly indicated gradual distancing of the emerging class of investors from the new issue market after the euphoria generated by the economic reform was over.

In the secondary market the Sensex had tremendous ups and downs during the period 1992-93 to 1996-97. The Bombay Stock Exchange Sensex reached the historic peak of 4467.32 on April 22, 1992 on the wings of a speculative frenzy. After the financial irregularities and the nexus of bankers and brokers were detected the Sensex went down to 2036.8 in April, 1993. But , as the economic atmosphere was hopeful, the Sensex again started gaining new heights and in September 1994 it touched the all time high of 4630.5. But the atmosphere of hope did not last long and the market could not sustain the trend. By January 1996 the Sensex touched the low of 2979.3. During 1996-97 the Sensex moved between the high of 3906.72 and the low of 2918.68. In the first few months of 1997-98 the B.S.E. Sensex showed an upward trend and it crossed the magic figure of 4000 in June 1997 and after reaching 4276.31 in August, 1997 again started declining. "The large annual variations in the Sensex indicate the volatility of the share prices and the unsustainable nature of growth of the capital market since 1992-93".[10] The volatility of the share prices, as shown above, clearly indicates that the market has failed to capture the uncertainties of the future and hence not efficient.

Economic reform is basically a long term and all pervading process of change. Hence, in order to pave the way for such a reform necessary change in the regulatory framework must be introduced. Under the situation the following suggestions are made:

i) credit rating of the issuing corporation should be made an integral part of every issue; ii) the disclosure and investor protection guidelines should be made more stringent and non-compliance of such guidelines should be made punishable offence; iii) guidelines for Merchant Bankers should be reformulated in the context of the experiences gained; iv) pricing of issues should be adjusted fully against both internal and external risks of the project; v) mutual funds should be allowed to play more dynamic role in the growth of capital market. Organisation of mutual funds may be made on corporate form instead of in the trust form; vi) in the context of the internationalisation of capital markets, the regulatory framework should also be made internationally compatible; vii) market for derivatives should be opened in India as in the developed markets of Europe, America and Japan, as an hedge against market risks; viii) last but not the least, steps should be initiated for reducing the stakes of foreign institutional investors in the portfolio of Indian companies. Because, the FIIs are playing havoc in the secondary market and thereby driving out the Indian investors from the arena of capital market.

REFERENCES

1. Simon M. Keane : *Stock Market Efficiency Theory, Evidence and Implications.* Heritage Publishers 1983. New Delhi, p.9.

2. Michael Firth : *The Valuation of Shares and the Efficient Market Theory.* The Macmillan Press Ltd., 1993, London, p.2.

3. Mohanty Basudev : *"Slump in Securities Market. Problems and Strategies for Its Sustainable Growth"* in Economic and Political Weekly Vol. XXXII. No. 42, Bombay, October 18-24. 1997. p. 2733.

4. Fama, E. : *"Efficient Capital Markets : A Review of Theory and Empirical Work".* Journal of Finance. May, 1970.

5. Simon M. Keane : *Op cit.* p. 12.

6. Praxis Consulting and Information Services Pvt. Ltd. : *The Prime Directory 1997,* New Delhi, p. 0-29.

7. Ibid., p. 0-32.

8. Ibid., p. 0-40

9. Ibid., p. 0-29.

10. Mohanty Basudev : *Op. cit.,* p. 2735.

Depository Services in India

Dr. R.L. Hyderabad*

INTRODUCTION

With the liberalisation of Indian Economy and introduction of financial sector reforms in 1991, the capital market has been growing by leaps and bounds. India now boasts of a large number of shareholders and also the largest number of listed companies in the world.[1] In terms of market capitalisation, which is the aggregate of the products of share prices of listed companies and the number of shares outstanding in each case, India has 19th rank in the world with a value of $ 128 billion in 1997 and in terms of turnover ratio, value of shares traded as per cent of capitalisation, of 42 per cent is placed at 15th position in the world.[2]

The primary market has become a prominent supplier of fresh capital. There has been more than thirty-fold increase in the funds raised during 1984 and 1993. In 1984, the capital issues amounted to Rs. 9. billion, while in 1993 it was Rs. 290 billion. The amount of capital issues increased to Rs. 395 billion in 1994 and Rs. 492 billion in 1995.[3] In 1996, despite depression in the market, Rs. 291 billion was collected and in 1997-98 an amount of Rs. 332 billion was mobilised.[4] Even FDI inflows into the country have shown a tremendous leap over the last few years. A total of Rs. 1,58,765 crores of FDI found its way into India in the period 1991-98, of which about Rs. 40,470 crores was from USA.[5]

* Reader, Department of Studies in Commerce, Karnatak University, Dharwad - 580 003 (Karnataka State)

The secondary market has also witnessed phenomenal changes during the same period. There are now 22 Stock Exchanges in India with 6,800 listed companies, BSE itself accounting for nearly 50 per cent of listed companies.[6] The National Stock Exchange (NSE) has started functioning with its screen based and scripless system. The establishment of Over The Counter Exchange of India (OTCEI) in 1992 is another milestone in the development of stock market in India.

Paradoxically, the problems of settlements on account of increase in volume of business are also on the rise. Investors, both individuals and institutions, have to experience a lot of inconvenience in effecting registration of securities in their favour and to ensure that they receive their rightful share of dividend, bonus, rights and other benefits.[7] Instances of bad deliveries, forged/fake signatures and certificates, large amount of paper work at company and brokers levels, long delays in settlement, etc., are other associated problems of large volume of business. Apart from these market risks, the foreign investors have objected against the undue delay which occurred in registration and FIIs have been representing to the Government to introduce scripless trading.[8]

In this scenario, it was felt that the setting up of a depository and the introduction of scripless settlement would improve the efficiency of the market, thus eliminating the various problems brought about by dealing in physical certificates. The Government of India promulgated the Depositories Ordinance in September, 1995, for the establishment of depositories in India. The Depositories Act was also passed in May, 1996 and the SEBI issued SEBI (Depositories and Participants) Regulations, 1996 to govern the working of depositories and their participants. The National Securities Depositories Limited (NSDL) was registered on 7th June, 1996 with the SEBI as the India's first depository.

CONCEPTUAL ISSUES

Depository system is a process of dematerialisation by which physical certificates of an investor are taken back and are destroyed /cancelled and an equivalent number of securities are credited in the electronic holdings of that investor. This dematerialisation of certificates is done by an independent agency called as depository and its participants. All the changes in the ownership of a security are effected through book/electronic entries only. Thus, depository system makes a departure from the existing physical trading to scripless trading. As a result of dematerialisation, securities become fungible, which means that all the holdings of a security will be identical and interchangeable as they will not have any unique characteristics such as distinctive numbers, certificate numbers or folio numbers.

The mechanism of depository system is similar to the operation of a bank account by an individual. While a bank performs the functions of holding, transferring and allowing withdrawal of funds; a depository performs the functions of holding, transferring and allowing withdrawal of securities.[9] An investor who is interested in dematerialisation has to open an electronic account with the depository participant of his choice and surrender share/bond certificates. The dematerialised scrips will be credited to his account by the participant and all changes will be recorded through electronic medium only.

The process of dematerialisation involves the following parties:

1. depository;
2. depository participants;
3. company/issuer of certificates; and
4. investor.

The Depository Act, 1996, defines depository as a body corporate authorised by SEBI to do the business of depositories. In other words, depository is an organisation where the securities are held in the electronic form at the request of the shareholder through the medium of depository participant. In the books of companies, the depository name will be recorded as the 'Registered Owner' of the securities.

A bank reaches out to the masses by setting up its branches; similarly a depository reaches out to the general investor through its agents who are the depository participants. These depository participants function like branch offices of a bank. They are the intermediaries between the investors and the depository. Investors have no direct access to the depository. Securities are credited to the respective electronic accounts of the investors by the participants and the balance is intimated from time to time. Public Financial Institutions, Scheduled Banks, RBI approved Foreign Banks operating in India, State Financial Corporations, Certified Custodians of

Securities, Clearing Companies of Stock Exchanges, Registered Stock Brokers, NBFCs, etc., can become depository participants.[10] The depository has to lay down the criteria for selecting the participants and the list has to be forwarded to the SEBI for its approval. If approved and registered by the SEBI, the depository participant can be admitted on to the depository.

Company or issuer of certificates cancels the certificates and the holdings are recorded in the name of the depository.

Under the Depositories Act, 1996, the investor has the option to opt for either physical certificates or demat scrips. If he opts for the latter, the securities are allotted to the depository and the list of allotees is given to the depository for its record keeping. However, the shareholder continues to be the 'beneficial owner ' of the securities and the term 'beneficial owner' has been defined by the Act as a person whose name is recorded as such with the depository. He continues to enjoy the benefits/ rights of a shareholder of a company, i.e., right to vote, right to receive dividend, bonus shares, rights issue, right to pledge or hypothecate securities, right to sell or transfer, etc. Further, the investor has the option to opt out of the dematerialisation process at any time and he will be issued back the physical certificates. This process of converting demat scrips into physical certificates is called as 'rematerialisation'.

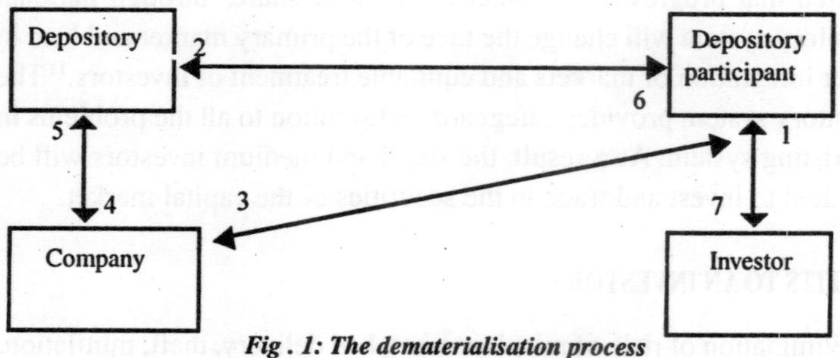

Fig . 1: The dematerialisation process

In brief, the following steps are involved for joining the system:

1. Investor has to approach a depository participant of his choice and open an account by surrendering the certificates.

2. Depository participant sends electronic message to the Depository of the request of the investor for dematerialisation.
3. He also intimates to the company and the certificates are sent to the company for confirmation and cancellation.
4. Company confirms the request from the Depository.
5. Company cancels the physical certificates and records the name of the depository as the 'registered owner'.
6. Depository completes the dematerialisation process and credits the account of the investor and informs the participant.
7. Depository participant, in turn, updates the account and informs the investor.

Like the bank branch office, the participant will issue a pass book or statement of holdings from time to time. The bonus shares, rights, etc., are credited to the electronic account and the dividend received is credited to the bank account of the investor. In case of any discrepancy in the statement of holdings, the investor can contact participant or depository for corrections. The act provides for indemnifying the investor for any loss caused due to the negligence of the depository or its participants.

BENEFITS OF THE DEPOSITORY SYSTEM

The dematerialisation process has advantages for all the parties involved in the capital market operations and for the capital market in general. It is expected that progressive dematerialisation of shares through national depository system will change the face of the primary market and lead to greater integration of markets and equitable treatment of investors.[11] The depository system provides safeguard and solution to all the problems in the existing system. As a result, the small and medium investors will be motivated to invest and trade in the securities of the capital market.

BENEFITS TO AN INVESTOR[12]

(i) Elimination of risk of misplacement, bad delivery, theft, mutilation, forged scrips, etc.

(ii) Reduction in transaction cost on account of scripless trading, lowest transaction cost at stock exchange levels and exemption of stamp duty

(iii) Registration of changes in ownership of securities is automatic because of payment versus delivery system followed in the depository system.

(iv) There is greater transparency and disclosures, wider liquidity resulting into investor's increased confidence giving rise to higher turnover which ultimately causes growth in the form and size of capital market.

(v) No courier/postal charges.

(vi) Facility for freezing/ locking which enables an investor to make his account non-operational.

The issuer of securities gains much from the system of dematerialisation. The company absolutely dispenses away with the mind boggling record keeping. All these results in savings in cost, less pay package to employees, litigation cases, etc.

Brokers also gain from the depository system on account of reduction in office expenses incurred in servicing the investor clients. The problems on account of bad deliveries, delay in effecting transaction, loss of certificates, etc., are totally avoided.

However, the above benefits are only illustrative and not exhaustive. Once the system is adopted in financial market to the full extent, the entire community will be benefited in one way or other through its latent and patent impacts and linkage advantages.

Progress of Depository System in India

With a view to give fillip to the growth of capital market, the Government of India promulgated the Depositories Ordinance on 20th September, 1995 and enacted Depositories Act, 1996, with retrospective effect from 20th September, 1995. Further, the SEBI issued SEBI (Depositories and Participants) Regulations, 1996, to govern the working of the system. The Depositories Act provides for the establishment of multiple depositories in the country unlike the western countries which have opted for a single national level depository.

The National Securities Depositories Limited (NSDL) was promoted by three major institutions in India—UTI, IDBI and NSE of India Ltd., on 7th June, 1996, as the India's first depository. The SEBI allowed NSDL to commence business from November, 1996. Since its establishment, the NSDL and the SEBI have embarked upon the task of popularising the dematerialisation process in the country. When NSDL operations began in November, 1996, only ten companies had signed up, offering to dematerialise their shares (at the option of the investors) and among them only three actually implemented.[13] At present a total of 228 issuers have entered into agreements with NSDL to get their securities dematerialised as on August 24, 1998. Amongst these, dematerialisation facilities were available for shares of 212 corporates.[14]

Amongst the companies which have opted for dematerialisation include popular corporates like ACC, BPCL, CRISIL, HDFC, ICICI, L and T, RIL, Siemens, Ashok Leyland, ITC Agrotech, Sesa Goa, Wockhardt, Pentafour, WIPRO, IndusInd Bank, Shree Cements, etc.

The number of depository participants has also shown an increasing trend and the total number of depository participants as on August 24, 1998 was 61, of which 30/35 are brokers while remaining are banks, custodians, etc.[15] About 184.8 crores shares, having a total value of over Rs. 27,000 crores have been dematerialised as on May 20, 1998. This has increased to over 256 crores shares with a total value of Rs. 40,900 crores by the end of July 1998, thus showing an increase of about 51 per cent in the value of shares dematerialised. As of July end, a total of 51, 492 investor accounts have been opened with the depository participants of NSDL. These accounts have been opened from 563 cities across the country and 35 cities from abroad. Maharashtra State tops the list with investor accounts of 16,298.[16] The companies which have crossed 20 per cent dematerialisation as a percentage of the market capitalisation are shown in Table—1.

The Table—1 clearly shows that dematerialisation is taking strong roots in Indian capital markets. The dematerialised scirps, though representing a small portion of the total number of listed stocks, accounted for more than 50 per cent of market capitalisation of all stocks, showing that bigger and bigger traded companies had opted for dematerialisation.[17]

Further, the SEBI has made it compulsory for institutional investors, which include FIIs, Mutual Funds, financial institutions and banks, dematerialised trading in 110 scrips.[18] Further, the SEBI has announced on August 19, 1998, in a press release that all settlements of trades done on an exchange in securities of 10 companies must be in dematerialised form from January 4, 1999.

TABLE—1
Dematerialisation as a Percentage of Market Capitalisation (in Excess of 20 per cent)

Name of the Company	per cent of dematerialisation
IndusInd Bank	**59.93**
WIPRO	**57.89**
Infosys	**39.10**
ICICI	**36.16**
Krishna Filaments	**26.55**
RIL	**25.86**
Shree Cements	**23.55**
Usha India	**21.54**
Larsen and Tubro	**21.20**
TISCO	**20.51**

Source : The Hindu, May 20, 1998, p. 19.

These 10 companies include SBI, ICICI, HDFC, L and T, BPCL, Infosys, IDBI, BSES, BOI and IndusInd Bank.[19]

CONCLUSIONS AND SUGGESTIONS

An analysis of the progress of dematerialisation process in India shows that depository system has slowly and steadily taking firm roots in the capital market. However, one need not be complacent. The percentage of companies which have opted for demat scrips forms miniscule percentage. Hence, NSDL and SEBI have to make concerted efforts in enlisting the support of companies and investors in total dematerialisation of investment and trading activities in securities. The following few suggestions will go a long way in percolating the system.

(1) The advantages of the system should be brought to the notice of investors especially the small and medium investors who are shy of investing in demat scrips. Appropriate publicity strategies are called for on the part of NSDL and SEBI.

(2) The operation of dematerialisation process is similar to the bank account. Hence, banking institutions with wide spread branch network

can be roped in as depository participants. Further, banks are looking for diversified activities/services to augment their income, improve their profitability and remain liquid due to competitive banking environment. The depository participants would be an attractive ancillary business for them in future and this will also build the investors confidence.

(3) The cost of dematerialisation process has to be minimised. The effective and economical services will entice both investors and companies in opting for the services.

(4) The dematerialisation should be made compulsory not only in respect of few scrips and institutional investors but also for other scrips and individual investors and companies within a certain time-frame. In fact dematerialisation should be one of the conditions for listing of securities by the exchanges.

(5) The efficiency of the system depends upon the electronic communication system. The automated data processing systems should be adopted and be connected among themselves by the depository, participants, companies and exchanges. A step in this direction has already been taken by establishing National Electronic Settlement and Transfer (NEST). Further, appropriate data processing system with necessary security features has become one of the conditions for selecting securities for dematerialisation.

(6) The NSDL from time to time release the names of registered depository participants with whom the investors have to open the account. A strict vigil over the working of these participants will build the confidence among the investing public.

(7) The cases of discrepancies due to negligence, fraud, etc., should be probed without any delay. Adequate compensation should be made payable to the aggrieved party by the NSDL or the SEBI. This will boost the investors confidence in the system.

(8) The SEBI and the Government should permit the dematerialisation of Government securities and securities of the PSE as they are the largest players in the financial market.

REFERENCES

1. Garg, R.K., *Depository services for the growth of capital markets in India*, Journal of Accounting and Finance, Vol. XI, No.2, Fall, 1997, page 184.

2. The Hindu, Bangalore Edition, August 3, 1998, page 20.

3. Pandey, I.M., *Keynote Address at National Seminar on Financial Services,* Dr. B.R. Ambedkar Open University, Hyderabad, 15th and 16th March, 1997, page 5.

4. The Hindu, Bangalore, August 17, 1998, page 18.

5. The Hindu, Bangalore, June 20, 1998, page 18.

6. Dr. Kumar, V.K., *The Emerging Indian Market for Global Portfolio Management,* Management Accountant, Vol. 31, No. 1, January, 1996, page 17.

7. *Introduction to Depositories,* A Booklet of NSDL, Mumbai, 1997, page 1.

8. Dr. Sarkar, A.K., *Indian Capital Market : Recent Development and Their Implications,* Management Accountant, Vol. 32, No.3, March, 1997, page 179.

9. *Introduction to Depositories op. cit.,* page 3.

10. Garg, R.K., *op. cit.,* page 186.

11. Bhave, C.B., Managing Director, NSDL, *quoted in The Hindu,* Bangalore, April 24, 1998, page 20.

12. Verma, J.C., *Manual of Merchant Banking,* Bharat Law House, New Delhi, 1996, page 1488.

13. The Hindu, Bangalore, April 24, 1998, page 20.

14. Bhave, C.B., Managing Director, NSDL, *Interview given to Deccan Herald Daily,* Bangalore , Aug 24, 1998, page 17.

15. Deccan Herald, *op. cit.,* page 22.

16. Deccan Herald, *op.cit.,* page 17.

17. The Hindu, Bangalore, April 24, 1998, page 20.

18. The Hindu, Bangalore, July 20, 1998, page 18.

19. The Hindu, Bangalore, August 20, 1998, page 18.

Managing Exchange Risks —An Indian Perspective

Yogesh Upadhyay *
Dr. S.K. Singh **

The terms of sovereignty of state have changed from the number of colonies at command and armed forces to the favourable balance of trade and economic prosperity. Before 1991, the country's economy was marked by protectionism and since then, liberalisation has become a buzz word. Indian has also become signatory to World Trade Organisation pact making inevitable to take the competition at global level head on.

The exporters and importers try to ensure that their level of profit and cost respectively, are not offset by the unfavourable change in the value of currency. As, in India the rate of exchange is partly determined by the rules of market. Therefore, chances of loss due to unfavourable volatility in the value of foreign currency can't be ignored.

The following articles sums up the measures and analyse their suitability in Indian context to manage exchange risk involved in the foreign exchange transactions.

A new economic era has arrived. The world is quickly becoming economically integrated, forcing unprecedented changes at every level of industry. Companies, small and large, are facing record levels of foreign competition for domestic and international market share. And the

* Incharge and Lecturer, Faculty of Commerce, Mahatma Gandhi Chitrakoot Gramodaya University, Chitrakoot, Satna (M.P.).

** Lecturer, Institute of Commerce and Management, Jiwaji University, Gwalior (MP).

proliferation of trade agreements and trade blocs among countries is not only increasing the complexity of international trade but also heightening the level of competition.

Nearly a decade after the phrase "global marketing" came into vogue, the world's largest consumer companies are coming to terms with what it really means. Marketing guru Theodore Levitt first coined the phrase in 1983, arguing that consumers around the world were beginning to have more and more alike.[1] As their tastes converged, the argument went, brands, products, and compaigns would become increasingly uniform, allowing global companies to benefit from cost efficiencies as they sold the same product the same way all over the world. He wrote:

"The world is becoming a common marketplace in which people-no matter where they live desire the same products and lifestyles. Global companies must forget the idiosyncratic differences between countries and cultures and instead concentrate on satisfying universal drives."

In an effort to gain secure and preferential access to foreign markets and in turn achieve a higher degree of economic security while maneuvering into the twenty-first century, effectively managing international financial risk has become essential for export-oriented firms and a mainstream need in the market place. Accelerating international receivable and managing international credit risk are increasingly viewed as a variation on domestic collections and credit management. On the sale side, more and more firms now use trade finance as just another tool to sell their goods, often providing an increasingly important advantage over competitors.

As the international trade increases, the economic importance of exports grow and competition increases, customers are requiring more sophisticated and competitive trade finance solutions. To defend market share and customer base, and more importantly, to be proactive in meeting these needs, it is essential to:

1. understand how international trade agreements, emerging trade blocs, and global trends will impact customer base;
2. identify and assess target market's international opportunities, risks and finance needs in this environment;

3. target the international niche that matches the firm's competitive strengths and appetite for international risk;
4. deliver timely, cost-effective solutions.

In an effort to increase the competitiveness, many countries have entered into trade agreements with one another. From 1947 through 1994, a total of 108 regional trade agreements were notified to the General Agreement on Tariff and Trade (GATT), the international body that governs approximately 90 per cent of world trade. Some of these agreements are between two countries; others are among many, creating trade blocs.

As growth in exports acclerates and global competition intensifies, the focus should be on the markets best for firms. The markets can be identified in a number of firms. The markets can be identified in a number of ways. Companies, for example, can be classified by their size (small, medium or large) or by their geography (e.g., those located in different regions). They can be identified by their industry, by their needs. They can even be categorised by their target export or import markets or developing countries. Another approach is to evaluate the revenue potential of the different market categories sorting by a variety of criteria. After analysing the firm's market, find the best match between the firm's international risk appetite, resources and target market. Whatever markets the firm chooses to target, delivering timely, cost-effective needs-based solutions is the key.

The demand for new and more creative financing by companies of all sizes will continue to increase. Offering trade finance solutions to meet these needs can be a defensive strategy to prevent competitors from making inroads in a firm's customer base and market place. To compete in this increasingly demanding environment, banks must first identify and focus on their preferred international market niche. Identifying the right niche may require more than one method of analysis.

Understanding trade finance needs is vital if many of the firm's customers export to developing countries, for example, and the firm wishes to keep the competition at bay and increase its value to these companies. It is important to understand the obstacles they face. For example, a real impediment to selling to companies in developing countries is the buyer's difficulty and expense in obtaining financing to pay for imports. By assisting developing country importers with liberal payment terms. Exporters can often export more of their products.

This strategy is becoming more important because of the exponential increase in global competition. Exporters that can manage risks and move quickly to arrange financing at attractive rates will win the business. Increasing competitive pressures, changing market environments, and new information processing technologies are allowing bankers to offer new financial products and services. In order to effectively provide additional, value-added services, commercial banks must better understand the needs of the customers they serve and develop products to meet these needs. In developing these services, it is important to remember that banks are shifting emphasis from activities related to deposit intermediation to the business of managing risks. Unfortunately the values of today's currencies oscillate widely, to the despair of international companies that want to plan ahead.[2]

THE ECONOMIC CONSEQUENCES OF EXCHANGE RATE CHANGES

The general concept of exposure refers to the degree to which a company is affected by exchange rate changes. Growth in international business has made more firms susceptible to exchange rate risk. Foreign exchange rate risk is a result of unexpected currency fluctuations that affect the value of the firm (i.e., the net present value of its cash flow streams). This risk arises whenever firms transact business in more than one currency. Thus, exposure to exchange risk can occur when settlement for a transaction is in a foreign currency.

Transaction Exposure

Transaction exposure arises out of the various types of transactions that require settlement in a foreign currency. Unexpected variability in cash flows caused by fluctuating currency exchange rates is a result of the firm's transaction exposure.

Operating Exposure

A real exchange rate affects a number of aspects of the firm's operations. An important factor is its pricing strategy. In international market that a firm tries to ensure that:

1. Its margins remain intact in home and abroad in all currencies;
2. Successfully save its margins as competition with foreign low-priced-goods intensify;
3. Pricing strategy of the firm which can provide a cushion to adjust exchange risk.

Accounting Exposure

Accounting exposure is the result of translation of foreign operations form local currencies involved to home currencies. It arises whenever a company is committed to a foreign currency-denominated transaction. Here the assets and liabilities of foreign subsidiaries are converted form the foreign currency to the domestic currency, by way of an accounting translation process that reflects one of several exchange rate adjustments. As a result, the values of assets and liabilities can change, thus affecting the consolidated financial settlements of the parent corporation. In short, both transaction exposure and translation exposure contribute to foreign exchange risk.

Here, attempt has been made to analyse the tools available and application thereof, to manage transaction exposure.

Tools to Manage Transaction Exposure

This process of risk reduction is called *hedging*. Essentially, hedging involves assuming risks that counterbalance on the risks that one is attempting to avoid. Hedging a particular currency exposure means establishing an offsetting currency position such that whatever is lost or gained on the original currency exposure is exactly offset by a corresponding foreign exchange gain or loss on the currency hedge.[3] Regardless of what happens to the future exchange rate, therefore, hedging locks in a home currency value for the currency exposure. In this way, hedging can protect a firm from unforeseen currency movements. There are costs to hedging. Businesses must determine their risk tolerance levels and the amount they are willing to spend to hedge a unit or risk. Once the amount they are willing to spend to hedge a unit of risk. Once the amount of risk that a business wants to hedge has been determined, the next step is to identify the instrument to be used to reduce the unwanted risk. These instruments are commonly referred to as derivatives.

A derivative is a financial contract whose value is derived from an underlying asset or index. There are several types of derivatives, including forward contracts, futures, equity swaps, interest rate swaps, and options. While each of these instruments can play a role in minimising risk, forward contracts, currency futures, currency options and currency swaps are most often used in mitigating foreign exchange rate risks. The table given below gives an account of the most common derivative instruments used to hedge against foreign exchange risk.

MARKET FOR SELECTED FINANCIAL DERIVATIVE INSTRUMENTS

Instruments	Notional amounts outstanding					
	1990	1991	1992	1993	1994	1995
	in billions of US dollars					
Exchange-traded instruments	2290.4	3519.3	4634.4	7771.1	8862.5	9185.3
Interest rate futures	1454.5	2156.7	2913.0	4958.7	5777.6	5863.4
Interest rate options	599.5	1072.6	13850.4	2362.4	2623.6	2741.7
Currency futures	17.0	18.3	26.5	34.7	40.1	37.9
Currency options	56.5	62.9	71.1	75.6	55.6	43.2
Stock market index futures	69.1	76.0	79.8	110.0	127.3	172.2
Stock market index options	93.7	132.8	158.6	229.7	238.3	326.9
Over-the-counter instruments	3450.3	4449.4	5345.7	8474.6	11303.2	17990.0
Interest rate swaps	2311.5	3065.1	3850.8	6117.3	8815.6	—
Currency swaps	577.5	807.2	860.4	899.6	914.8	—
Other swap-related derivatives	561.3	577.2	634.5	1397.6	1572.8	—

(1) Calls and puts, (2) Data collected by the International Swaps and Derivatives Association (ISDA) only; the two sides of contracts between ISDA members are reported once only. (3) Adjusted for reporting of both currencies; including cross-currency interest rate swaps. (4) Caps, collars, floors and swaptions.

Source : Futures Industry Association, various Futures and Options Exchanges, ISDA and BIS calculation adapted from V.K. Bhalla, "Global Trade Financing and Use of Derivatives in Volatile Forex Market," Chartered Secretary, July 1997, p. 779.

In a complex and rapidly evolving financial environment the banker can develop new relationships and strengthen existing ones by becoming familiar with these instruments and how they work to reduce foreign exchange rate risk. To conclude, growing recognition of the economic benefits of derivatives markets, a better understanding of such instruments and more prudent use of them means closer competition and greater management responsibility against actual or potential risks.

Forward Market Hedge

In a forward market hedge, a company that has sufficient foreign currency will sell foreign currency forward, whereas a company that is in short of foreign currency will buy the currency forward. In this way, the company can fix the selected currency value of foreign currency cash flow.

Currency Futures

In 1972, the Chicago Mercantile Exchange opened its International Monetary Market (IMM) division. The IMM provides an outlet for currency speculators and for those looking to reduce their currency risks. Trade takes place in currency futures, which are contracts for specific quantities of given currencies; the exchange rate is fixed at the time the contract is entered into, and the delivery date is set by the board of directors of the IMM. These contracts, which represented the first step in the development of financial futures, are pattered after those for grain and commodity futures contracts, which have been traded on Chicago's exchanges for over 100 years.

Currency futures is just like any other future deal, where an agreement is entered to buy or sell a standard object of value on a future day at a rate (price) agreed between parties through a transaction in an organised market. The unique feature is that it is a future deal in a specific currency. Such currency futures (CF) are transacted on the floor of an organised Future Exchange. Though forward exchange and CFs contract look similar. Some differences could be enlisted below:

- Forward exchange enjoys a global market where banks and financial institutions form the basic players. CFs, however, are traded only on certain floors of specified exchanges. Chicago, New York, London, Tokyo and Singapore happens to be some of the important floors where currency futures are traded.
- Forward Exchange uses sophisticated trading system using electronic and satellite media GLOBEX, an electronic Mercantile Exchange System (introduced in 1992), whereas in currency futures, open outcry in the pit of the aforesaid Exchange is still practised.
- Forward exchange contracts have tailor made contract size for customers. But in currency contracts, contract sizes are standardised.

The Chicago currency futures exchange (the largest amongst the CF exchanges) are mentioned in Table given below:

CONTRACT SIZE FOR CURRENCY FUTURES IN CHICAGO FINANCIAL FUTURE EXCHANGE[4]

Exchange		Contract size
Pound Sterling	£	25,000
Canadian Dollar	C$	1,000,000
Deutsche Mark	DM	1,25,000
Dutch Guilder	DG	1,25,000
Franc (France)	FF	12,50,000
Yen (Japan)	V	1,25,000
Franc (Swiss)	SFr	1,25,000
Mexican Peso	Peso	10,00,000

- Forward contracts are very flexible in terms of their maturity or delivery time or date. But, in case of CF, maturity and delivery has been standardised. They fall on 10th March, June, September and December i.e., every quarter of a calendar year.
- Forward contracts are settled through contracts with banks, whereas CFs are settled through a clearing house especially set up for the purpose.
- Leverages tend to be high in CFs. However, in case of forward there are no such leverages and such contracts are based on client-bank relationship.
- CFs are extremely liquid because of standardised contracts in comparison to future context.
- Last but not the least, is the question of credit risk. In case of CFs, the credit risk is borne by the clearing house where the contract is executed. This is not the case of forward exchange contract. Under forward contract, the counterpart entering the agreement generally bears the risk.

Money Market Hedge

An alternative to a forward market hedge is to use a money market hedge. A money market hedge involves simultaneous borrowing and lending activities in two different currencies to lock in a specific currency value of a future foreign currency flow.

The equality of the net cash flows from the forward market and money market hedges is not coincidental. The interest rates and forward and spot rates were selected so that interest rate parity holds. In effect, the simultaneous borrowing and lending transactions associated with a money market hedge enable a concern to create *homemade* forward contract. The effective rate on this forward contract will equal forward rate if interest rate parity holds. Otherwise, a covered interest arbitrate would exist.

Risk Shifting

Selling companies tries to avoid the risk of transaction exposure altogether by asking the counterpart to price the order in the home currency of the selling company. Despite the fact that this form of risk shifting is *zero-sum game*, it is common in international business. Firms typically attempt to invoice exports in strong currencies and import in weak currencies. Though, it not possible to gain form risk shifting if one is dealing with informed customers or suppliers.

Pricing Decisions

In case of credit sales made overseas, the general rule is to convert the home currency and the import country's currency by using the forward rate, not the spot rate. If the exporter's currency price is high enough, the exporter should follow through with the sale. Similarly, if the dollar price on a foreign-currency-denominated import is low enough, the importer should follow through on the purchase. This is keeping in view that the price of currency is volatile.

Exposure Netting

Exposure netting involves offsetting exposures in one currency with exposures in the same or another currency, where exchange rates are expected to move in such a way that losses (gains) on the first exposed position should be offset by gains (losses) on the second currency exposure.[5] The assumption underlying the exposure netting is that the net gain or loss on the entire currency exposure portfolio is what matters, rather than the gain or loss on any individual monetary unit.

Companies practice multicurrency exposure netting all the time.

In practice, exposure netting involves one of three possibilities:

1. A firm can offset a long position in a currency with a short position in that same currency.
2. If the exchange rate movements of two currencies are positively correlated (for example, the Swiss franc and Deutsche mark,), then the firm can offset a long position in one currency with a short position in the other.
3. If the currency movements are negatively correlated, then short (or long) positions can be used to offset each other.

Currency Risk Sharing

In addition to, or instead of, a traditional hedge, the currency risks associated with the contract can be shared by the companies involved. Currency risk sharing can be implemented by developing a customized hedge contract imbedded in the underlying trade transaction. This hedge contract typically takes the form of a price adjustment clause, whereby a base price is adjusted to reflect certain exchange rate changes. Here, as the base price crosses a limit, then only the parties would share the currency risk. The neutral zone represents the currency range in which risk is not shared.

Currency Options

Whatever advantages the forward or the futures contract might hold for their purchaser, they have a common disadvantage. While they protect the holder against the risk of adverse movements in exchange rates, they eliminate the possibility of gaining a windfall profit form favorable movements. This was apparently one of the considerations that led some commercial banks to offer *currency options* to their customers. Exchange-traded currency options were first offered in 1983 by Philadelphia Stock Exchange (PGLX).

Currency options (COs) are the rights given to the buyers of foreign currency to buy (call) or sell (put) a specific amount of foreign currency at a specific exchange rate (the strike price) till a specific date when the contract expires. The seller of the put option or call option must fulfill the contract if the buyer so desires it. Because the options not to buy or sell has value, the buyer must pay the seller of the options some premium for this privilege. An *American options* can be exercised at any time up to the expiration date; a *European option* can only be exercised at maturity.

Options are purchased and traded either on an organized exchange (such as the PHLX) or in the over-the counter (OTC) market. Exchange-traded options or listed options are standardised contracts with predetermined exercise prices, standard maturities (one, three, six, nine and 12 months), and fixed maturities (March, June, September, and December). Options on the PHLX are available in the ECU and seven currencies—Deutsche Mark, Pound Sterling, French Franc, Swiss Franc, Japanese Yen, Canadian Dollar, and Australian Dollar—and are traded in standard contracts half the size of the IMM futures contracts. Other organized option exchanges are located in Amsterdam (European Stock Exchange).

Table given below enlists the standardized currency options in Philadelphia Exchange.

CURRENCY OPTIONS CONTRACT SIZE FOR VARIOUS CURRENCIES PROVIDED BY PHILADELPHIA EXCHANGE[6]

Exchange		Size Per Contract
Australian Dollar	A$	50,000
Pound Sterling	£	31, 250
Canadian Dollar	C$	50,000
Deutsche Mark	DM	6,200
Franc (France)	FF	2,50,000
Yen (Japan)	V	62,50,000
Franc (Swiss)	SFr	62,500
European Currency Units	ECU	62500

In many circumstances, the firm is not sure whether the hedged foreign currency cash inflow or outflow will materialize. For example, a company X GE learned on January 1 that it had won a contract to supply boilers to Y. But suppose that although X's bid on the contract was submitted on January 1, the announcement of the winning bid would not be until April 1. During the three months period from January 1 to April 1, X does not know whether it will receive a payment of DM 25 million on December 31 or not. This uncertainty has important consequences for the appropriate hedging strategy.

Company X would like to guarantee that the exchange rate doesn't move against it between the time it bids and the time it gets paid, should it win the contract. Until recently, X or any company that bid on a foreign contract in a foreign currency and was not assured of success would be unable to resolve its foreign exchange risk dilemma. The advent of currency options has changed all that. Specifically, the solution to managing its currency risk in this case is for X, at the time of its bid, to purchase an option to sell DM 25 million on December 31. For example, suppose that on January 1, X can buy for $ 1,00,000 the right to sell Citibank DM 25 million on December 31st a price of $0.3828 per Deutsche mark. If it enters into this option contract with Citibank, X will guarantee itself a minimum price ($9.57 million) should its bid be selected, while simultaneously ensuring that if it lost the bid, its loss would be limited to the price paid for the option contract (the premium of $ 1,00,000). Should the spot price of the Deutsche mark on December 31 exceed $0.3828, X would let its option contract expire unexcercised and convert the DM 25 million at the prevailing spot rate.

Two types of options are available to manage exchange risk. A *put* option, such as the one appropriate to X's situation, gives the buyer the right, but not the obligation, to sell a specified number of foreign currency units to the option seller at a fixed dollar price, up to the option's expiration date. Alternatively, a *call* option is the right but not the obligation, to buy the foreign currency at a specified dollar price, up to the event its bid is rejected. A put option is required when the party requires foreign exchange. By buying a put option the party sells the domestic exchange to procure the right amount of foreign exchange at a specified rate. The reverse is done, when payment is needed to be done by the party. A call option is entered so that foreign exchange can be bought by exchanging the domestic currency.

Relevance to India

Many exporters lack a complete understanding of the foreign exchange risk associated with this new global era. In India, the bankers provide additional, value-added services to these exporters by helping them understand the nature of their foreign exchange rate risk and assisting them in developing and implementing appropriate strategies to minimise these risks.

Use of derivatives or hedging instruments does not seem to be very attractive in India. This may be due to lack of flexibility in such future contracts, especially in terms of settlement date and contract size.

Besides, the commercial banks in India provide for forward contracts quotations for upto a year and also provide hedge against the currency rate fluctuations. This makes the future contract lack luster to Indian firms. The fact remains that, the over the counter forward contracts covered by the banks are more convenient to the firms.

Sooner or later, as the rupee is made fully convertible at current as well as capital account, the use of derivatives to manage exchange risk shall become inevitable.

CONCLUSION

Derivatives are not available to Indian firms. This is because they come within the ambit of the foreign exchange regulation and require governments approval. The other side of the picture remains that, such instruments are lack-lusture before the ever competing commercial banks who provide over the counter facilities with better forward contracts. However, as the country is moving towards globalisation and the foreign banks entering into every sphere, the business sooner or later shall join the global current.

REFERENCES

1. "*Global Marketing With A Pinch Of Local Salt*", Economic Times, Ibid, p.6.

2. The Economist, May 28, 1988, p. 81.

3. Alan C. Shapiro. *Multinational Financial Management*, Printice Hall of India Pvt. Ltd., New Delhi, 1996, p. 201.

4 Abhijit Dutta, "*Currency Futures and Currency Options: Innovations in International Money Market*", Chartered Secretary, May, 1996, p. 483.

5. Alan C. Shapiro, *Ibid.*, p. 201.

6. Abhijit Dutta, *Ibid.*, p. 484.

SOME OTHER SELECTED REFERENCES

1. Cornell, Bradford, and Alan C. Shapiro, "*Managing Foreign Exchange Risks*", Midland Corporate Finance Journal, Fall 1983.

2. Dufey, Gunter and S.L. Srinivasulu, "*The Case for Corporate Management of Foreign Exchange Risk*", Financial Management, Summer, 1984.

3. Giddy, Ian H., "*The Foreign Exchange Option as a Hedging Tool*," Midland Corporate Finance Journal, Fall 1983.

4. Shrinivasulu, Sam and Edward Massura, "*Sharing Currency Risks in Long-Term Contracts*", Business International Money Reports, February 23, 1987.

5. *Using Currency Futures and Options, Chicago*: Chicago Mercantile Exchange, 1987.

6. Garman, Mark B. And Steven W. Kohlhagen, "*Foreign Currency Option Values*", Journal of International Money and Finance, December, 1983.

Buy-Back of Shares by Companies in India

Dr. Omprakash Kajipet *

The proposal for allowing buy-back of shares by companies in India has been in the debate for quite some time in the context of re-enacting the Companies Act of 1956. The proposal of buy-back of shares needs to be examined carefully in the back-drop of liberalised, fast changing and highly competitive business environment. In addition, its relevance may have to be looked at, from the point of view of revival of sluggish capital market, liquidity to dormant shares, safeguarding the interest of small investors from the evils of free pricing of capital issues, financial restructuring of corporate bodies and defending against hostile take-over bids.

This article attempts to analyse and examine the important aspects of buy-back of shares with special emphasis on financial restructuring.

POSITION IN INDIA

The Companies Act of 1956, at present, does not permit a company to buy-back its own shares. As per section 77 (1) of the Companies Act 1956, a company cannot purchase its own shares and further it states that —"No company limited by shares and no company limited by guarantee and having a share capital, shall have the power to buy its own shares, unless the consequent reduction of capital is affected and sanctioned in pursuance of Sections 100 to 104 and Section 402 of the Act.

---

* Associate Professor of Commerce, Department of Commerce and Business Management, Satavahana Post-graduate College, Kakatiya University, Karimnagar-505 001 (A.P).

Sections 100 to 104 of the Companies Act specify that— "a company can reduce its share capital to the extent of shares not paid-up, cancel share capital which is lost or is unrepresented by available assets or reduce shares which are in excess of the requirement of the company". This is subjected to the confirmation of the court of the special resolution reducing the share capital.

Section 402 of the Companies Act, however empowers the Company Law Board to allow a company to buy-back its shares only in cases of "mismanagement" and/or "oppression".

The restrictions on buy-back of shares by companies in India are mainly to protect the interests of small investors from price rigging and insider trading by vested interests and also to safeguard the interests of long-term creditors in the matters relating to repayment of loans and interest on such loans.

POSITION IN ADVANCED COUNTRIES

The buy-back of shares by companies was in practice and viewed as a common strategy in advanced countries like USA, UK, and Canada. In these countries, companies utilise their reserves to buy-back equity shares either for the purpose of extinguishing the share capital or for treasury operations.

The buy-back of equity shares in the first case results in the reduction of paid-up capital, and consequently higher earnings and book value per share and ultimately the market price of equity goes up. The reduction of share capital usually strengthens the promoters control and enhances the value of equity shareholders.

In case of treasury operations, Companies buy their shares from open market and keep these as treasury stock. This results in a diversion of company's funds to buy shares and reduction in the value of equity for shareholders and also helps the promoters to strengthen their control over the shares bought back, without any investment of their own.

In the USA, the practice of buy-back of shares by companies is a common business strategy to utilise surplus and idle funds, after paying dividends in order to achieve a reduction in equity and to increase earnings per share and market price.

There are two methods of buy-back of shares quite popular in the US. The first method is to buy-back shares in the open market. Under this method, the company first makes a public announcement to repurchase its own securities in the market and on the basis of the offers received, it can buy shares at the best market price. This method of share buy-back gives companies flexibility of making purchases through any broker so that the purchases do not disturb the share price. In the other method of share buy-back, a general tender offer to all shareholders is made by the company to repurchase a fixed amount of its securities at pre-stated price. The price is generally 15 per cent higher than the prevailing market price of securities on the day of the general tender.

There are two main legal safeguards in the matter of buy-back of shares in the US. First, a company cannot repurchase its shares in the open market within a year of capital issue so as to prevent the company from jacking up the price of its securities in the stock market at the time of public offer. Second, the volume of shares repurchased on any day in the capital market cannot exceed five per cent of the trading volume of the share on the particular day.

In the UK, the Companies Act 1985, empowers the Secretary of State to make regulations enabling a company to purchase its own shares. The purchase is of two types—'market purchase' and 'off-market purchase'. Market purchase includes any purchases of listed shares and those dealt in on the unlisted securities market whereas off-market purchases as a purchase of any other type of shares.

A Company can make market purchase of its own shares provided the purchase has been authorised by a resolution of the shareholders in general meeting specifying the maximum number of shares to be purchased, the maximum and minimum price for said purchases, and the time limit within which the purchase has to be completed.

A company may make an off-market purchase by a specific contract which has received advance authorisation by a special resolution of shareholders. The shareholders, whose shares are being purchased, are not allowed to vote on a special resolution to avoid conflict of interest.

On completing the purchase transaction, the company has to file a return with the Registrar, stating all the details like the number and nominal value of shares purchased, the date on which the purchases were completed and the amount paid on such purchases.

The law and procedure relating to buy-back of shares by Companies differ from country to country. It is considered that the legal system in the USA and Canada is quite liberal, but in the UK there is an elaborate procedure for buying-back of shares by the companies.

CURRENT SCENARIO

There has been a lot of debate in recent times in India over the proposal of buy-back of equity shares by Companies as a part of the re-enactment of Companies Act of 1956. The Report of the Working Group on the Companies Act 1956, contains a recommendation as to buy-back of their own shares by companies from investors, and to restructure their capital structure subject to certain provisions. As a result, the new Companies Bill, 1997, also contains a clause permitting companies to buy-back their own shares subject to certain rules and safeguards.

The working Group has suggested that the proposal for buy-back of shares shall be subjected to the following provisions:

1. A special resolution by shareholders, clearly specifying (i) the amount allocated for buy-back; (ii) time period for completing buy-back operations; and (iii) the funds allocated for buy-back from "free reserves" and share premium account.
2. No issue of any new shares including right issues but excluding bonus issues for a period of 12 months from the completion of buy-back operations.
3. The buy-back of shares and consequent extinction of share capital should not lead to an increase in debt-equity ratio in excess of 2:1.
4. In case of buy-back of shares for treasury operations, such shares will not be reissued for 24 months after the last date of buy-back, and will be subjected to various restrictions as far as voting and dividend rights and entitlement to rights and bonus shares are concerned.

5. In case of off-the market buy-back from specific class of shareholders, the potential sellers will not have voting rights on the special resolution.
6. The buy-back decision shall be accompanied by a "declaration of solvency" by the Board, signed by the Managing Director and atleast one more Director of the company, which will be in force for one year after the buy-back.
7. Any deviation from such compliance will be subjected to substantial fine and/or imprisonment.

There has been a sharp response from the Indian Corporate sector to the proposal for buy-back of shares in general and the legal provisions suggested in this regard by the Working Group in particular. Though many promoters have welcomed the proposal and intended use it as an instrument to induct some life into their earnings per share and market price of shares, some have expressed contentions over the following.

1. In case of buy-back for extinction of share capital, the restriction on norms of debt-equity ratio is practically not possible and difficult to be followed by many industries, as the debt-equity ratio differ from one industry to another and they require different debt-equity ratios for optimum utilisation of resources. Hence, the restriction on debt equity ratios needs to be dropped.
2. In case, the object of buy-back of shares is to block hostile take-over bids, the restriction of no voting rights on shares bought-back may not serve the purpose effectively. Though the promoters proportionate voting power increases marginally as a consequence of the reduction in overall voting capital, but the cost of this can be very prohibitive. Thus, the voting rights on shares bought-back should not be extinguished.

BUY-BACK OF SHARES AND COMPANIES BILL, 1997

The Companies Bill, 1997 introduced in Rajya Sabha on August 14, 1997, which seeks to recast company law in tune with the changing economic environment, to respond to the changing corporate practices, incorporate appropriately the concepts developed in the international corporate market, protect the rights and interest of investors, creditors and other parties, contains a clause dealing with buy-back of securities.

Clause 69 of the Bill, a refinement over the clause 68 of the Draft Companies Bill, permitting the Indian companies to buy-back their own securities subject to certain rules and regulations. According to this clause, there will be no re-issue of shares or other securities purchased by a company and such shares are to be cancelled. Further, buy-back of shares for treasury operations as envisioned in the Draft Bill has been given up. Under the provisions, buy-back operations can be undertaken under a special resolution. The shares or other securities may be purchased from:

(i) the existing holders of securities on a proportionate basis; or
(ii) the open market; or
(iii) the odd-lot shareholders in the case of public listed company; or
(iv) the shares alloted to employees in pursuant to a scheme of stock option ; or
(v) the classes of shareholders through negotiation or other arrangement.

However, in case of buy-back through negotiation or other arrangement, the stipulation is that no votes are cast in favour of the special resolution by those whose shares to be purchased.

The need for buy-back is still an open ended issue, as the necessity for resorting to buy-back will have to be spelt out in the resolution of general meeting. In other words, the Board of Directors will have to decide the necessity for the buy-back and the majority decision of the Board is enough for the purpose. However, there is a need to prescribe unanimous vote of the Directors present at the meeting or two-thirds majority so that a proposal of this type enjoys the support of greatest number of Directors.

ARGUMENTS IN FAVOUR OF BUY-BACK

The proposal of buy-back of shares by Indian companies can be favoured based on the following advantages.

A Method of Corporate Financial Restructuring

Corporate restructuring signifies reorientation reorganisation, or realignment of assets, investments, and liability structure through conscious actions with a view to alter drastically the quality and quantity of the future cashflow streams. In India Corporate restructuring is still in its adolescent stage and so is the status of regulatory framework which has not yet completely evolved and is characterised by fragmentation, where several statutes and regulatory bodies have a role to play in the regulation of corporate restructuring.

Financial re-structuring also called capital re-structuring, is very much an essential consideration in any type of re-structuring. But in many cases of restructuring decisions, only this aspect of restructuring is given importance and remains as a core area of re-structuring. The buy-back of shares as a method of corporate financial restructuring is very popular in countries like USA and UK to bring in gains in the shape of increased earnings per share, higher prices (P/E ratio) to the investors.

A recent study by the JP Morgan, US Investment Bank, of share buy-back programmes in Europe, shows that they provide significant excess returns to shareholders and can lead to longer-run uplift in valuation of shares. It is found that the larger the share repurchase programme, the more were the gains for shareholders, both in terms of price and earnings. The findings of this study support the argument that investors prefer companies to use excess cash or debt capacity to re-structure their financial structure through share buy-back, rather than retaining with them, and that cash is worth more in the hands of the shareholders than it is on the balance sheet.

An Armoury against Hostile Take-overs

Buy-back of shares can be a good defence measure against take-over bids. However, it should be noted that share buy-back if improperly used, can be very prohibitive in terms of cost. As per the provisions of the Companies Bill, 1997, the promoters holding will rise only by a fraction of the number of shares acquired. For every Rs. 100 paid to acquire shares, the voting power of the promoters will increase only by a few rupees worth.

The reason for this is that the shares acquired, by the company are not added to the promoters voting power. On the contrary, these are required to be extinguished. However, shares buy-back can, in appropriate circumstances, may be found useful. Therefore, the need for buy back provision is no doubt necessary particularly in the context of new take-over code, though buy-back can be resorted to for a variety of other reasons, other than preventing hostile take-over of companies.

A Tool for Revival of Capital Market

The current state of the capital market is very much discouraging. The factors mainly responsible for the sluggish conditions in the capital market are malpractices in capital issues, misuse of free pricing regulation, price rigging and insider trading.

Since, the abolition of the Office of the Controller of Capital Issues and introduction of free pricing of the capital issues by companies, the conditions in primary market got deteriorated. The reason is that the promoters have floated their public and rights offers with hefty premium to mobilise larger funds without any costs. They got succeeded in their objective at the cost of confidence of small investors in the corporate capital issues. Thus, with introduction of shares buy-back provision, the corporate bodies can make an attempt to instill confidence in the investors through buy-back of their own shares at reasonable and justifiable levels of price, which are otherwise being traded at large discounts from their offer prices.

The share buy-back may also help in providing the much needed liquidity to the dormant shares on the stock market on account of reduction in equity, improved earnings per share and the higher market prices, the likely consequences of buy-back of shares by companies. Therefore, shares buy-back if properly used, it works as a tool for the revival of the capital market from the sluggish conditions.

Buy-back of shares once introduced legally that will fulfil the long-pending demands of the industrialists. Further, it may also provide advantages not only to companies, and also to the investors, customers, and the economy at large.

Arguments against Buy-back

The proposal of buy-back of shares is opposed to in some sections of the society as it affects the interests of the common investors because of the following:

a) The promoters may likely to adopt unhealthy practices in buying back shares through negotiations/ arrangements. Prices of shares may be rigged heavily to favour a group of sellers. The shady deals may take place to benefit the promoters. In the process the genuine investors may stand to loose in terms of depletion / exhaustion of company's reserve funds, consequential reduction in the rates of dividend or pricing of all future share issues at exorbitant prices.

b) The buy-back of shares by companies may induce the directors / finance executives/ employees, who possess price sensitive information, to resort to "insider trading" to the detrimental to the interests of small investors, and which is often regarded as a direct fall-out of the buy-back of shares.

c) The buy-back of shares may prove to be costly and less productive to combat the hostile take-over bids, in case the shares bought back carry no voting rights as proposed in the new Companies Bill, 1997.

It is thus, argued that "buy-back" may lead to unhealthy, unscrupulous, and unfair market practices like–price rigging, shady deals by promoters, and insider trading, as a consequence the common investors would suffer. Besides, it cannot be an effective means to defeat the hostile take-overs under the proposed new Companies Bill, 1997.

AUTHOR'S VIEW

After having examined the various aspects relating to the issue of buy-back of shares, it clearly emerges that the proposal has certain definite advantages and relevance especially in contemporary times of liberalisation and integration of domestic with global markets and institutions. At the same time, like many measures, it is too, not free from certain fall-out affects. Because of fear of such affects, it is not wise to refrain from permitting the buy-back of shares by companies in India, atleast keeping the experience of other advanced countries in view in this regard. However, while permitting the buy-back by Indian companies, the following checks and safeguards would make the proposal more effective in the attainment of desired advantages.

i) Effective check and supervision by SEBI over insider trading by the directors /executives / employees etc., before and immediately after buy-back operations.

ii) Stringent actions/penalty/fines against the persons indulged in insider trading, once the fact of insider trading is established.

iii) Knowledge and approval of financial institutions, banks, and other long-term creditors, who got substantial stake to the proposal, prior to buy–back of shares by such companies.

iv) Transparency in buy-back operations needs to ensured. The companies proposing to buy-back of their own shares should be required to notify and give wide publicity of all the details like number of shares to be repurchased, the price of repurchase, the time limit to complete buy -back and methods/ procedures of buy-back operations.

v) Ceiling/restriction on the volume of shares repurchased on any day in the capital market and also within a year of capital issue to prevent the company from jacking up the price of its securities in the stock market, as prevalent in the US.

Human Resource Accounting–Need for Standardisation of HRA Practices in India

Anjali Paul *

P.D. Saini **

The traditional accounting system is based on certain conventions and principles which have evolved over a period of time as a consequence of social, economic, political and legal influences. The adherence of some of these conventions and practices in India limits the usefulness of accounting as a tool for decision making in certain areas. One such example is that of the human resource. Inspite of the technological advancement and increasing importance of computerisation, human resources continue to play a dominating role in the effective use of physical and financial resources. The limitation of the traditional accounting in this regard has led to the development of a new field of inquiry in accounting called Human Resource Accounting; which seeks to identity and measure data about human resources and communicates the information to management and other users of accounting information.

The present study is designed to highlight the challenges confronted by the Organisation in adopting HRA and the need for the Standardisation of HRA practices in India.

WHAT IS HUMAN RESOURCE ACCOUNTING?

Human Resource Accounting is "a process of identifying, measuring and communicating information relating to human resources in order to facilitate effective management with in the organisation." Thus HRA is

* Lecturer, Deptt. of Accountancy and Law, Faculty of Commerce, Dayalbagh Educational Institute, Dayalbagh, Agra.

accounting for people as an organisational resource. It involves measuring the economic value of people in organisation. The human resource accounting is more concerned with the decision making area of accounting. The American Accounting Association Committee on Human Resource Accounting has defined human resource accounting as:

"Human Resource Accounting is the process of identifying and measuring data about human resources and communicating this information to the interested parties."

It helps in developing financial assessments for the people with in the organisation and monitoring of these assessments in the light of set accounting policy of the concern from time to time. The purpose of HRA is to improve the quality of human resources decisions made both internally and externally concerning an organisation. The specific objectives of HRA may be outlined as:

- to develop methods of measuring human resource cost and value;
- to monitor the effectiveness of the management's utilisation of human assets;
- to furnish cost value information for making management decision about acquiring, allocating, developing and maintaining human resources in order to attain cost effective organisational objectives, and
- to provide a sound and effective basis of asset control.

CHALLENGES

In the process of introducing HRA, management is often confronted with the following challenges, as the methods followed for adopting HRA suffer from one or the other type of problem:

1. Though human capital plays an important role in any organisation, there is widespread disagreement regarding the recognition and valuation of human resources as asset, because an asset is one on which the entity should have legally enforceable claim or it should be owned by the entity. However, human resources hardly fulfil these norms. As such, the effort to recognise human resources as assets suffer a set back.

2. Proper matching of costs with revenue is not possible unless the costs on the recruitment, training and developing of personnel are capitalised over their effective service lives.
3. The very idea of showing human resources as an asset on the balance sheet of a firm tends to be aribitrary.
4. Another practical difficulty regarding HRA is quantification and pricing of employees in respect of jobs which do not yield any physical output. These practical difficulties are subject to the influence of age, qualifications, previous experience, point of first entry etc., etc.
5. In all the methods, the salaries earned by the employees are taken as the basis for valuing human resources. Thus the career movements of employees either with in the organisation or elsewhere in the other organisation is kept outside the purview of valuation.

HUMAN RESOURCE ACCOUNTING PRACTICES IN INDIA

The process of assigning cost and value to the human resources has evinced interest of some company managements in India. This is evident from a survey which shows the increasing trend in adopting Human Resource Accounting system in Indian companies. As there is no statutory requirement in India to publish Human Resource Accounting Information and also because the leading accounting of human resource cost and value data.

If we look at the annual reports of public enterprises and private enterprises in India we find that chairman's report invariably contains the statements highlighting the significance of human resources in their remarks that our employees are our most important asset and without their significant contribution, the present growth in the operation would not have been attained. " I wish to place it as record of my sincere gratitude for the hard work done by the employees of our company. These qualitative pronouncements reflect the importance of human resources in an enterprise but the quantitative information relating to their contribution or their value is nowhere recorded or shown in the financial accounts.

However, in practice, a few enterprises, stated below, value there human resources and report this information in their annual reports.

A) Public Sector Enterprises

- Bharat Heavy Electrical Limited
- Cement Corporation of India.
- Project and Equipment Corporation of India.
- Engineers India Ltd.
- Minerals and Metals Trading Corp. of India.
- Electrical India Ltd.
- Oil and Natural Gas Commission
- Hindustan Shipyard Ltd.
- Steel Authority of India Ltd.

B) Private Sector Enterprises

- Tata Engineering and Locomotive Works (TELCO)
- Associate Cement Company (ACC)
- Southern Petrochemicals Industries Corporation (SPIC)
- Infosys Ltd.

Methodology Used

The second part of this paper is devoted to study the HRA practices of selected companies in India and to build a case which shows the need of standardisation of such practices in India.

The above mentioned undertakings were scanned as per the rating of Economic Times and through a small questionnaire that was send to them. It was identified that out of them 12 were found publishing such information in their annual reports in supplement form and the remaining two organisations has historical cost based system designed to generate output for internal decision making only.

A pre-tested questionnaire was administered to the managers, who actually operated the HRA system of fourteen organisations to collect detailed information regarding the operational part of the system. It was found that all of the organisations which published HRA information used the Lev and Schwartz model of economic value using an employee's anticipated future earnings as a sarrogate of his value.

The practices of all the organisations regarding accounting of their human resources were studied but the practices of only four of them are analysed here.

ANALYSIS AND FINDINGS

Company EC : Company EC is an engineering organisation. It was the pioneering organisation in installing HRA system in India in mid 70's. Its HRA system is based on the modified version of the model proposed by Lev and Schwartz. The system provides value of human resources grouped in six categories.

Salary is the base used by EC for determining the value of it's human resource. The mean of the grade is taken to plot the salary level in each grade, where salary includes both direct and indirect variables. The average salary is projected till retirement, taken into consideration the increments as per the terms of the grade and the possibilities of carrier growth. To account for the increment factor a weightage goes up to 1.25. To take into account the carrier growth of employees, carrier chart is prepared. The carrier chart shows that in the years to come how many vacancies will arise at each level/rank in the organisation and also which level/rank employees will be promoted. The company provides weights for efficiency also. The process of providing weights for efficiency follows a set pattern every year irrespective of the category of the employees. In the very first year, EC provides such weight of 95 per cent and gets reduced by 5 per cent every year till it reaches 75 per cent.

The projected salary stream is discounted at 12 per cent rate. The rationale of using this discount rate is that it is the rate which EC uses as the minimum rate of return in it's capital budgeting decisions.

Company OL: Company OL is engaged in exploration, drilling and production of oil. It values it's human resources on the basis of the Lev and Schwartz model taking salary as base. The system generates single absolute figures of value and does not provides categorised value of its human resource. Salary again includes both direct and indirect expenses. The expenditure on its employees as shown in its audited accounts is taken as the starting point since it represents the actual amount paid. The projection of expenditure on employees is made at a compound rate of 10 per cent for every four years and at 25 per cent for every fifth year. The rate of 10 per cent purports to take care of the increase in salary because of price rise and increments. The rise of 15 per cent represents the impact of pay revisions on the salary bill, as oil has a policy to revise pay every five years.

The projection of salaries is made for the period of 20 years and not upto the retirement age. The projected salaries streams is discounted at a rate of 12.25 per cent as this rate represents the rate at which the Government of India advances the latest loan to oil.

Company MT: Company MT organise and undertakes the exports from India of minerals and ores. It values its human resources by using Lev and Schwartz model. The final output of the system is presented in two categories, viz., officers and staff. The organisation has actually grouped the employees in fourteen categories while carrying out the valuation exercise. Salary is used a basis of valuation which include both direct and indirect benefits.

The salary stream is projected upto the retirement age of 58 years by loading the average salary at a rate of 10 per cent every year, which takes care of increments and price rise, for all categories of employees except chairman and directors whose salaries are projected on the basis of actual increments likely to be given during their association with the organisation.

The valuation period is taken to be the difference between the retirement age and the average age. The average age is calculate for each level/rank.

The projected salary scheme is discounted at the rate of 12 per cent to calculate its present value. The rate being the required rate of return used by the Government of India and by the company in evaluation of capital budgeting proposals.

Company PC: Company PC is engaged in the manufacture of chemicals and petrochemicals. It uses Lev and Schwartz model to value its human resource with certain modifications. The value of human resources is published in the annual reports classified in six categories.

The valuation process is salary based. The weighted average annual gross salary is computed along with the weighted average age and the number of employees for each category. The salary stream is projected up to the retirement age. While projecting the salaries and annual increment factor is taken into account. The possibility of promotion of its employees based on the general promotion policy of the company. The projected salary stream is discounted at the rate of 17 per cent, i.e., it's weighted average cost of capital to calculate the present value of human resource.

NEED FOR STANDARDISATION OF HRA PRACTICES

The study of the HRA systems of the four organisations provides an overview of the wide variations that exist in the practices followed to the human resources. Though the organisation followed the economic value approach and used the Lev and Schwartz model yet the process of accounting for the human resources differed considerably.

Salary is used as a surrogate for value by all the organisations assuming that employees will contributes at least equal to the salary paid to them. The mean of the grate is taken, as it is difficult to carry out the valuation exercise on the basis of actual salary level. But the process of calculating mean salary differs. Though most of the organisations have calculated simple mean, Company PC uses the weighted average salary as a surrogate of value.

The valuation period for which the salaries are projected represents the time span for which the employees are expected to stay with the organisation. The final value calculations depend much to the length of the valuation period. But the practices vary widely. Company EC prepares a career chart and on the basis of the same determines the valuation period. Company OL has assumed the valuation period of 20 years arbitrarily. Company MT and Company PC use average age for the determination of valuation period.

The projection of salaries for the duration of valuation period requires two variables. Firstly, what will be the pattern of movement of employees, i.e., whether employees will continue to occupy the present position or will they be promoted. Secondly, at what rate incidence of increase in salary due to increments and inflation should be taken. As regard the possibility of promotion, most of the organisations have assumed that employees will continue to occupy the same position at which they are at the time of valuation. Such an assumption is in-built in the Lev and Schwartz model. But Company PC and Company EC have considered the possibility of promotion. As regards the second variable, i.e., the rate of increment of salary, different organisations have used different rates.

For example, Company EC used the rate of 5 per cent which is not compounded annually. Company OL uses 10 per cent for every four years (compounded annually) and 25 per cent for every fifth year.

To discount the projected salary stream to calculate the present value, again different organisations use different rates. Company PC uses the discount rate of 17 per cent, which represents its overall cost of capital. Company EC and Company MT use 12 per cent discount rate, as such rate represents the minimum rate of return used in their capital project evaluation processes. Company OL uses 12.25 per cent rate which happens to be rate at which the Government of India extended the latest loan to it. Further the use of the same cut off rate for the evaluation of human capital projects as used for the evaluation of physical capital projects is conceptually wrong and questionable.

Company EC has considered a discounting factor on present value of salaries to account for efficiency. No other organisation has followed such a practice.

CONCLUSION

The human resource accounting differ considerably in India. Though the model used by various organisations to account for human resources is the same, i.e., the Lev and Schwartz model is operationalised differs widely. There is no uniformity of practices regarding calculation of mean salary, determination of expected tenure, projection of salary-stream for the tenure and the calculation of present value using a discount rate. It is suggested that the professional accountancy bodies like the Institute of Chartered Accountants of India and the Institute of Cost and Works Accountants of India should take more active interest in the subject and take steps to develop and recommend a uniform approach to human resource accounting.

REFERENCES

Albanese, Robert, *Managing Toward Accountability for Performance*, Richard D. Irwin Inc., Homewood, Illinios, 1978.

Brummet, R.Lee, Flamholtz, Eric G., Pyle, William C., *Human Resource Accounting : Development and Implementation in Industry*, Braun and Brumfield, Michigan, 1969.

Elaxes, Alexander V., *Human Capital Approach to Economic Development*, Metropolitan Book Co., New Delhi, 1983.

Flamholtz, Eric G., *Human Resource Accounting*, Dickinson Publishing Co., Encino, California, 1974.

American Accounting Association, *Accounting Review Report of the Committee on Accounting for Human Resources* Supplement. Vol. 49, 1974.

A.N. Khandelwar, *Rationale of HRA*, The Chartered Accountant, July 1979.

Alexander, M.O., "*Investment in People*" Canadian C.A., July 1971.

Das Gupta N., *Financial Reporting in India*, Sultan Chand, New Delhi, 1988.

Annual Reports of Companies using HRA.

Economic Times

Tax on Distributed Profits (TDP) — Some Implications

Dr. H.M. Jha 'Bidyarthi'*

ABSTRACT

Introduction of the scheme of "Tax on Distributed Profit" at a flat rate of 10 per cent since June 1, 1997 is a step towards removing double taxation of dividend income, rewarding companies ploughing back greater part of its annual profits and encouraging small investors to join capital market. And hence the scheme has been with a very high enthusiasm in the trade and industry circle. But on its implementation side it has raised many serious implications, as pointed out in this paper, like double and triple taxation on dividend income of US-64 and inter-corporate investments, increase in cost of capital and tax burden of the company, mullifying the advantage of reduced corporate tax rates, erosion of capital, change in financial statements etc. etc. To be truly meaningful the scheme needs some fundamental revisions as suggested in this paper such as TDP at a rate commensurate with the dividend pay-out ration and not amount of dividend, exemption to the inter-corporate investments etc.

The landmark budget presented in Lok Sabha on 28th Feb., 1997 by Mr. P. Chidambaram, the then Finance Minister of India for the year 1997-98 didn't seem to remain merely a budget for '97-98 but through its most sensitive, very innovative and visionary provisions it was to leave a permanent scar on the life and health of all sections of the society. In the business and industry sector, people virtually ran out of adjectives to praise

* Assistant Professor, SSGM College of Engineering, Shegaon (Maharashtra)

the budget. Not that many of their suggestions had found merit in the eyes of Mr. Chidamabaram—the architect of that budget—but had also been proposed in toto in that finance budget. One such proposal in that budget put an end to the vigorous debate of many years relating to the issue of tax on dividends by abolishing what was popularly criticised as "double taxation of dividends"—both equity and preference dividend. In turn TDP—Tax on Distributed Profit—has been introduced since then to replace TDS—Tax Deduction at Source—with reference to dividend income of the individuals.

PROVISIONS FOR TDP

In the part 'B' of the finance budget 1997-98 provisions for TDP were made vide Sections 100-101 as follows :

100) "Another area of rigorous debate over many years relates to the issue of tax on dividends, I wish to end this debate. hence, I propose to abolish tax on dividends in the hands of the shareholders.

101) Some companies distribute exorbitant dividends. Ideally, they should retain the bulk of their profits and plough them into fresh investments. I intend to reward companies who invest in future growth. Hence, I propose to levy a tax on distributed profits at the moderate rate of 10 per cent on the amount so distributed. This tax shall be an incidence on the company and shall not be passed on to the shareholder."

Accordingly changes in Income Tax Act were incorporated to give effect to these provisions.

MEANING OF THE PROVISION

For years together, governments had been unable to decide whether to tax profits in the hands of shareholders of a company or a company itself. Finally through the aforesaid provisions in the budget '97-98 the then Finance Minister took a plunge. He decided in favour of the perennial underdog—the small shareholders. Dividend is declared out of post-tax income of the company. Again it was subject to tax in the hands of the shareholders. Thus, dividend had been subject to double taxation. So while the shareholders earned high dividends all these years, they paid out a substantial share of those earnings in tax. Now they will earn lower dividends, but pay out a lower share of that income in tax. The system of taxing dividends in the hands of recipient has, therefore, been replaced by 10 per cent tax on profits distributed as dividend. The tax on dividend whether out of past reserves or current profits vide section 115-0 of Income Tax Act became applicable to all dividends declared or paid after June 1, 1997. In lieu of the budget proposals on TDP, this section of IT Act requires the company to pay tax at a flat rate of 10 per cent on the dividend distributed within fourteen days of its declaration. Failure to do so entails a levy of simple interest at 2 per cent for every month or part of the month against the taxes payable.

The initial reaction to the budget was one of jubilation. It was considered as a "bold and courageous bag of risky economic experiments and political gambles". The scrapping of tax on dividends was a gimmick as the government had merely transferred the onus of the tax from the shareholders to the company. The abolition of tax on dividends was however considered to provide a great psychological boost to the investor.

The Bombay Stock Exchange President Mr. M.G. Damani had said that three major proposals—abolition of double taxation on dividend tax buy back of shares and Modification of Alternate Tax (MAT) would go a long way in improving the bottom lines of corporate sector. The SEBI also felt that it was possible that companies might shy away from declaring dividends, given this new tax.

CONSEQUENCES OF TDP

Despite this bold announcement of the then Finance Minister, the end effect of this amendment might be mellowed down on account of levying tax of 10 per cent on the distributed profits (dividend) which shall now be an incidence of the company and shall not be passed on to the shareholders in order to reward companies which ideally retain bulk of their profits and plough them into fresh investment for future growth.

In all probability experts feel that the provision regarding TDP might, in the first place, induce companies to defer their annual accounts finalisation and declaration of dividend beyond May, 1997 i.e. in the year of introduction of the scheme. They further felt that the provision would attract promoters of closely held companies all the more since the entire dividend income was made tax free. Thus ,while the company would pay taxes, the promoters would enjoy the full kitty without having to pay a single rupeeas tax. This and many other effects of TDP would be seen in terms of the followings :

1. The structure of P & L Accounts of the company
2. The tax liabilities of the companies and its shareholders
3. Cost of equity and preference capital
4. Leverage analysis of the firm
5. Dividend policy of the firm
6. Capital market moods and temperament
7. Reworking of profits
8. Capital structure becoming more inclined towards debt capital as equity and preference capital has also created a permanent liability in terms of minimum fixed charges on it i.e. the TDP).
9. Ploughing back of profit (Accumulation of profit/issue of bonus shares /declaration of interim dividends etc.)
10. Govt. Tax revenues
11. Small investors v/s big investors of equity and preference shares
12. Dividend payment in the year of application of TDP provisions.

Mr. P.K. Sahu, a member of the expert group that proposed changes in the Income Tax Act regarding dividend tax marked a note of dissent. Mr. Sahu's note questions the group's proposal of a flat 10 per cent tax at source on income distributed by mutual funds to unit holders and income in the hands of unit holders to be exempted from tax. He said it would open up a bonanza for corporates who regularly invest surplus cash in the Unit Scheme 64 yielding 16 per cent income. Now it will be a tax free income of 14.4 per cent after allowing TDP of 10 per cent.

Accordingly dividend income by company shall be subjected to double taxation which was not existing before defying the very purpose of abolishing tax on dividend as shown below:

This note of dissent further says that the present scheme will be highly equitable as it may result in "higher profits making company" paying less tax than " lower profit making company" in another transaction.

Tax relief through TDP may not buoy companies after all. That budget also reduced tax on corporate sector from 43 per cent, including surcharge,

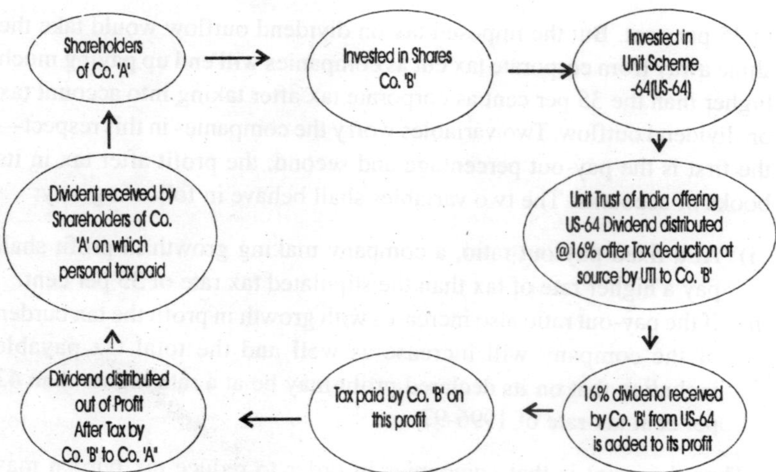

Fig. Showing Taxation during pre-TDP era

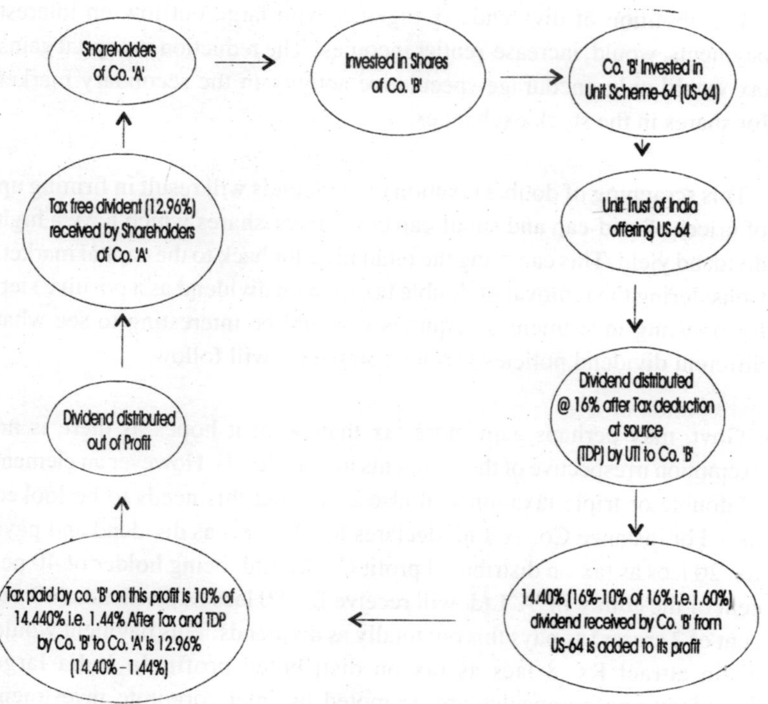

Fig. Showing Taxation during post-TDP era.

to 35 per cent. But the imposed tax on dividend outflow would take the shine away from corporate tax cut as companies will end up paying much higher than the 35 per cent as corporate tax after taking into account tax on dividend outflow. Two variables worry the companies in this respect—the first is the pay-out percentage and second, the profit after tax in its books of accounts. The two variables shall behave in following way:

i) At a fixed pay-out ratio, a company making growth in profit shall pay a higher rate of tax than the stipulated tax rate of 35 per cent.
ii) If the pay-out ratio also increases with growth in profit the tax burden of the company will increase as well and the total tax payable including that on its declared profit may be at a rate higher than 43 per cent tax rate of 1996-97.

Thus the point is that companies in order to reduce tax burden may reduce dividend, even though they do have adequate positive NPV projects in hand to justify the higher retained earnings.

The abolition of dividend tax together with large outflow on interest payments, would, increase 'rentier incomes'. The reduction in capital gains tax would only encourage speculative activity in the secondary market for shares in the stock exchanges.

This scrapping of double taxation on dividends will result in firming up of prices of mid-cap and small-cap companies' shares which have a high dividend yield. This can bring the retail investor back to the capital market. Considering the removal of double taxation on dividend as a positive step for boosting investment on equities it would be interesting to see what different dividend policies various companies will follow.

Govt. may perhaps gain more tax than what it hopes as there is no exemption irrespective of the recipients income levels. However an element of double or triple taxation will also come and this needs to be looked into. For instance Co. 'A' Ltd. declares Rs. 2 crores as dividend and pays Rs. 20 lacs as tax on distributed profit Co. 'B' Ltd. being holder of 40 per cent of the equity of 'A' Ltd. will receive Rs. 80 lacs as dividends (40 per cent of 2 crores) as pays this out totally as dividends. This payment would again attract Rs. 8 lacs as tax on distributed profit. In India large manufacturing companies are promoted by inter-corporate investment firms. Further the recommendation in the report of the working group set up to recast the Companies Act, 1956, to permit companies to invest up to 60 per cent of their capital and free reserves in either inter-corporate loans or investments mean higher earning of the company by way of dividends received from such inter-investments and so higher tax incidence on dividend. So the tax on distributed profits would have a cascading effect.

There is an unintended consequence of the Finance Bill 1997 exclusively on the financial statements (for the year 1997-98) on account of tax incidence on distributed profits. The TDS on dividend was applicable till 31 March,'97, dividend received between April 1 and May 31, '97 will not get the benefit of section 80M and entire amount of dividend will be taxable and after June 1, '97 dividend will be received without TDS under TDP and thus on the closing date of the financial year i.e., March 31, 1998, depending upon the policy of the companies in the light of the aforesaid, other things remaining the same, the profitability shall vary for different tax considerations. This will all happen because of non-uniformity in the dates taken for effecting TDP (i.e. June 1, 1997) and withdrawal of sections 80M and 80L (i.e., April 1, 1997).

Since shareholders don't have to pay any tax on dividends received, companies with high dividends would become attractive. Several big corporations like Glaxo India (204 per cent), Punjab Tractors (125 per cent), Bajaj Auto (100 per cent), Hindustan Lever (100 per cent in '95-96) have higher pay-outs because of their large equity-base, but may not be now actually paying high dividends.

10 per cent TDP levied with the purpose of encouraging companies to reinvest their surplus back into the business may prove difficult for infrastructure companies like that of power sector as these are capital intensive and their return on equity is seldom high. This return will further go down on account of TDP. The IRR is barely the desired number as compared to the cost of capital and the opportunity returns. Added to this is the companies (Transfer of Profits to Reserve) Rules, 1975 according to which a certain percentage (based on the dividend declared) of the profits needs to be transferred to the reserves. If the company declares a dividend of over 20 per cent, in effect this leaves only 30 per cent of the profits to be distributed, as a dividend of 10 per cent needs to be transferred to reserves. TDP further reduces the distributable surplus to 81.80 per cent. This is a big blow to the power industry.

Change in the structure and content of financial statements of companies due to TDP is another implication of the scheme. It would now look like as follows :

Sales
Less Cost of Goods Sold
Gross Profit
Less Operating Expenses
Less Depreciation and Other Expenses
Profit Before Interest and Tax
Less Interest
Profit Before Tax
Less Tax on Profit Earnt
Profit Before Interest and Tax
Less Tax on Distributed Profit
Net Profit

REVISION OF TDP

In order to truly meet the objectives keeping which in mind Mr. P. Chidambaram, the then Finance Minister had provided for TDP there needs some modification/ revisions in this scheme as mentioned below :

1. If the motive is to tax those companies which distribute very large amounts as dividends, TDP should be levied on the basis of the rate of dividend and not on the quantum of dividend i.e. the dividend pay-out ratio.
2. From investors' point of view their returns are proportionate to the rate of dividend and they are not aware of the pay-out ratios. Therefore, it needs little sense to equate two sets of companies having two dividend pay-outs, say, 100 per cent and 20 per cent, for the purpose of calculating TDP.

Case Comparison

Particulars	Co.A Ltd (with low capital base)	Co.B LTD. (with high capital base)	Co. C LTD. (with high capital base)
Share Capital	Rs. 20 Crores	Rs. 500 Crores	Rs. 500 Crores
Profits	Rs. 15 Crores	Rs. 110 Crores	Rs. 110 Crores
Profitability	7.5 per cent	22%	22%
Dividend Payout %	50%	50%	90%
Dividend Amount without TDP	Rs. 7.5 Crores	Rs. 55 Crores	Rs. 90 Crores
Dividend Rate without TDP	37.5%	11%	18%
TDP	3.5%	1%	1.6% (approx.)
Dividend Rate After TDP	34%	10%	16.4%
Errosion of Dividend Rate by TDP	3.5%	1%	1.6%

3 Another remedial measure would be to differentiate between companies paying a large dividend in absolute terms and those which pay a higher rate of dividend. If the tax on dividend is to be there, it could probably be on a sliding scale mechanism as follows :

S.No.	Dividend Rate	TDP Rate
1.	1.10%	1%
2.	11.20%	2%
3.	21-30%	3%
4.	31-40%	5%
	41-50%	7%
6.	> 50%	10%

4. The other remedy is to link the transfer to reserves (retained earning policy) is percentage of profits, TDP is the percentage of the dividend paid. This would achieve the twin objectives of giving returns to the investors as well as maximise revenue to the exchequer through TDP. Following table shows this mechanism:

TDP - Transfer Percentage Link

S.No.	Dividend Payout %	Transfer Reserve %	TDP 10% of Payout	Balance Transfer %
1.	50%	10%	5%	5%
2.	60%	10%	6%	4%
3.	70%	10%	7%	3%
4.	80%	10%	8%	2%
5.	90%	10%	9%	1%
6.	>100%	10%	>10%	Zero %

5. Yet another remedy is to consider TDP as a charge to the P and L A/C and treat it as an expenditure so that the total tax paid by the company will get reduced.
6. Exemption of inter-corporate dividends from the 10 per cent tax on distributed profits in order to avoid double taxation, as demanded by the Associated Chambers of Commerce and Industry also.
7. By doing away Income Tax on dividend there will be savings of income tax for individuals and Hindu Undivided Family ranging from 100 per cent to 30 per cent depending upon income of the tax payers. Likewise the savings to corporate tax payers on their dividend income would be to the tune of 35 per cent. However, levying 10 per cent tax on distributed profit indirectly means that even after the reduced corporate income tax from 40 per cent to 35 per cent (43 per cent to 38 per cent in 1997-98, the total tax burden payable by the company making payment of dividend work out to about 45 per cent which appears to be on the higher side. TDP should actually be, to serious with double taxation problem, at a figure of just 5 per cent and not 10 per cent.

CONCLUSIONS

Obviously, therefore the introduction of TDP is a welcome step for the industry but not in the present shape as it leads to many discretionary consequences and also to scope of some serious loopholes as illustrated above. Instead a modified form of this scheme on the suggested lines would make it truly meaningful and purposed tool.

REFERENCES

i) The Economic Times, Daily Newspaper published by Times Group. New Delhi.
ii) The Financial Express, Daily Newspaper, published by Express Group, New Delhi.
iii) Chandra, Prasanna : "*The Financial Management (1997)*" Tata McGraw-Hill Publishing Co., Delhi.

Rationalisation of Income-Tax Law — Some Reflections

Dr M.M. Maji *

THE BUOYANCY AND IMPORTANCE OF INCOME TAX

The tax revenue occupied the most significant position in the Central Budget constituting 70 to 80 per cent of the total revenue receipts of the Government and nearly 15 to 20 per cent of the national income. Income tax together with customs and excise duties constitutes the principal source of tax revenue for the Central Government in India. Although it ranks below the other two in terms of revenue significance, income tax has a special place in the armoury of tax instruments of the Government. No other tax lends itself so well to serve the objective of equity as income tax, income being universally regarded as the best single index of economic power, and in the ultimate analysis, the acid test for the acceptability of a tax is equity. From the following table it will be clear that direct taxes as a source of revenue seemed to be diminishing. The major portion of the direct taxes is earned from corporation tax as corporation tax alone constitutes 75 to 80 per cent of total direct taxes and 10 to 14 per cent of the total tax revenue. Though the share of direct taxes was gradually declining, in the last two years (1995-96 and 1996-97) there has been increasing trend. Taxation being an economic tool, may be the Government have no better options but to apply its various features to suit to the total economic philosophy of the country as a whole from time to time. Income tax has become a powerful pan in the hands of the Indian political systems.

* Professor of Commerce, the University of Kalyani, Ex-Head, Dept. of Commerce, The University of Burdwan.

Taxes in India

Year	Direct Taxes	Indirect Taxes	Total	% of Direct Taxes of Total Taxes	% of Indirect Taxes of Total Taxes	% of Total Taxes of GDP
1950-51	230	430	660	34.85	65.15	6
1960-61	420	1,040	1,460	28.77	71.23	10
1970-71	1,100	3,590	4,600	23.91	76.09	14
1980-81	3,696	16,100	19,790	18.65	81.35	17
1995-96	39,780	1,32,220	1,72,000	23.13	76.87	20
1996-97	39,003	93,142	1,32,145	29.52	70.48	22

ATTEMPTS SO FAR MADE SINCE 1961 FOR SIMPLIFICATION AND RATIONALISATION OF TAX LAWS

The Income-tax Act 1961 of today is the product of the recommendations of the Direct Tax Enquiry Committee headed by Sri Mahabir Tyagi. The objective was to evolve laws that would least inconvenience the tax collection and tax compliance by the tax payers. These goal and attempts seemed to be widening from year after year. This 1961 Act underwent many changes based on the following : Bhoothalingam's Report 1967 (Rationalisation and Simplification of Tax Structure); Report on the working of Administrative Reforms Commission headed by Sri K. Hanumanthia; Wanchoo Committee Report, 1971 (Direct Taxes Enquiry Committee); C.C. Choksi Committee Report, (Direct Taxes Laws Committee), 1978; V.M. Dandekar Committee Report, 1980 (Expert Committee on Tax measures to promote employment); L.K. Jha Commission Report 1982-83 (Economic and Administrative Reforms); Raja Chelliah Committee Report, 1992 (Tax Reforms Committee) . The report of an expert group was submitted on Feb. 2, 1997 though very few recommendations of this group have been accepted. What for all these committees and commissions ? The ultimate goal is to have a simplified and ratioinalised tax laws so that there may not be any difficulty on the part of the assessees in complying with tax laws as well as on the part of the administration in enforcing the laws. But we have not yet got it, though the process is on.

SOME SPECIFIC POINTS TO BE NOTED IN CONNECTION WITH SIMPLIFICATION AND RATIONALISATION OF DIRECT TAX LAW

1. The existing system of highly progressive taxation has a deleterious effect on the economy and the society. A steeply progressive tax on income saps the incentives to save, to invest and to take risks. Equity also suffers when the tax rates are perceived as unreasonable and even the law abiding citizens resort to tax evasion with an easy conscience. This situation arises from the fact that the existing rates of taxation are higher than those prevailing in other developing countries. To mitigate the ill effects of progressive taxation, Government have been compelled to provide for preferential treatment for certain categories of income by way of incentives and granted concessions to diminish hardship but provisions for all these inevitably open up lapses and loopholes which are exploited more by resourceful taxpayers. In order to plug them anti-avoidance provisions have been made. The end result is that the tax laws become complicated beyond the understanding of the common assessees and even the tax advisers. Tax administration also feels it difficult to administer. This creates hatred among the assessees and the entire system is disrespected by the people. So the desired objectives are not fulfilled.
2. The Indian experience with income tax, in parallel with that of many a developing countries, bears ample testimony to the ill-effects of taxes that are equitable in intent but poorly administered. Realising this, along with other countries India has carried out radical reform of her tax systems and because of its high visibility income tax has come in the forefront of tax reform programme in India. Sweeping changes have been brought about by the Raja Chelliah Committee; the major thrust being towards a structure that has wide base but moderate rates. The results are hopeful. However, much remains to be done.
3. The ratio of income tax to GDP in India still remains low compared to that of other developing countries. An important reason for the relatively low income tax to GDP ratio is the exclusion of agricultural incomes from the purview of the Central income tax. But an equally persistent factor has been inadequate compliance. While there are no firm estimates, the proportion of income and activities that go unreported for tax purposes is widely believed to be large with adverse implications for equity and efficiency of the tax system as a whole.

4. Despite considerable research in this respect here and elsewhere, what induces the people to comply with tax laws still remains an enigma. Conventional wisdom has if that tax compliance depends much upon the efficacy of sanctions against non-compliance. However, sanctions prescribed in the law alone cannot ensure compliance unless there is a credible threat of being caught and punished in the event of default. Stiff penalties lose their teeth if detection is lax and conviction happens to be rare. Confiscatory penalties by themselves do not lend credibility. In fact, statutory penalties, if too stiff, often generate adverse reactions both among the people and the judiciary. Tax system which has been successful in securing high degree of compliance depends more on mechanisms which help detection, and a judicial process, which while assuring justice, does not allow defaulters to frustrate law through prolonged litigation. In a country like ours where corruption is endemic and the general attitude of the society towards tax evasion is permissive, simultaneously with fundamental reform of tax structure, radical reorganisation of tax administration also relying on computerised information system is necessary whereby information regarding transactions having tax implications are received automatically and recorded systematically with arrangements for retrieval whenever required.
5. There is also a growing recognition that along with sanctions for default, incentives for good tax payers' behaviour also can overcome people's antipathy towards taxes. A friendly rather than an adversarial tax department, willing to hear the other side with patience and understanding and provide facilities for compliance can go a long way to enhance respect for the law even on the part of habitual defaulters.
6. For any Act to be administrable and also acceptable to the people, simplicity of both structure and law is essential. Any attempt to reform the tax system or re-write the tax law has to keep in view the basic criteria of a good tax system, viz., equity, efficiency and simplicity. Of course the revenue aspect cannot be overlooked. Along with these basic criteria, the factor of administrative feasibility should also be considered. While no improvement is possible if the weaknesses of administration are taken to be irremediable, the limitations of the administration cannot also be brushed aside.
7. Problems arise when we try to adhere to all these criteria in equal measure, for there are complexities and trade-off, for instance, between simplicity and equity or equity and administrative ease.

Equity often demands fine tuning of the tax base that creates complications in law and administration. An additional source of complexity often is the attempt to achieve social and economic goals, i.e., the non-tax objectives through tax reliefs while the trend in recent years has been to steer clear of incentives in tax laws. There are certain basic economic and social objectives, which the tax system has to respect in the larger interest of the community. Nevertheless, there is considerable scope to simplify and rationalise the Income-tax Act. It should, however, be appreciated that tax laws cannot be simplified beyond a point. For there can be a conflict between simplicity and precision. Simplicity sometimes breeds ambiguity, providing scope for varying interpretation. Keeping this in mind reform should be made without making radical departure from the basic framework of the income tax law unless it was felt desirable in the interest of facility of understanding or administrative ease. Any substantial change in the language of the law or judicially noted or interpreted phraseology, may give rise to a fresh spurt of needless litigation with attendant uncertainty for the tax payer as well as for the Revenue.

SPECIFIC SUGGESTIONS FOR SIMPLIFICATION AND RATIONALISATION OF INCOME TAX LAW

In view of the above discussion, it may be suggested that the mode of computation of total income followed in India should be retained, viz., on global basis but computed under a few specified heads, such as, salaries, income from house property, profits and gains of business or profession, etc. within the small canvas of this article suggestions for simplification of laws for incomes under all the heads cannot be incorporated; so here only the valuation of long term capital asset and computation of long term capital gain have been taken for consideration.

In computing the cost of acquisition, where a capital asset was acquired by the assessee before the 1st of April, 1981, he has an option to substitute the fair market value of the asset as on 1st of April, 1981. In most cases involving old properties, the assessees generally opt for the substituted cost. But this generates disputes as valuation on a notional basis involves a large element of subjectivity. Seldom do the valuation reports of the registered valuer and the departmental valuer agree and the resultant disputes take a long time to settle through appeals. The designated date, 1st of April, 1981, was substituted for 1st of April, 1974 by the Finance

Act, 1992. Thereafter, the cost is indexed on the basis of a price index notified by the government every year, anchored to the Consumer Price Index (CPI).

In order to simplify the mode of computation of capital gains and eliminate the need for notional valuation, a new scheme proposed is as outlined below:

i. For assets, other than financial assets, held for more than eight years, 60 per cent of the sale proceeds will be deemed to be the cost of acquisition. The remaining 40 per cent will be taken to be the capital gain.
ii. For assets held for less than eight years but more than three years, the assessee will be allowed to claim 50 per cent of the sale proceeds as the deemed cost of acquisition.
iii. In both the cases, the assessee will be given an option to claim by way of deduction the actual cost of the asset together with costs of improvement to be supported with evidence.
iv. Assets held for a period of not more than three years will continue to be treated as short term capital asset and the gains on their transfer will be computed by allowing the actual cost of acquisition together with the cost of improvement, if any.

This scheme does away with the need for notional valuation on a designated date and for shifting the date periodically. There will be no need for inflation indexing either. An element of indexation is built into the deemed cost basis for the assets under (i) and (ii) above. For short term capital assets no adjustment for inflation is called for.

A further deduction of 50 per cent of the gains computed in the manner proposed above will be allowed and the resultant amount of capital gains will be included in the total income. This further deduction would obviate the need to have a special rate of tax on capital gains (which is currently 50 per cent of the maximum marginal rate) as the normal rate schedule applicable to the assessee's total income will apply.

The presumptive cost method outlined above may be questioned on grounds of equity as it does not allow explicitly for differences in the capital gain accruing to assessees transferring their assets on the same date and at the same selling price. For in the case of assets like urban property value appreciation varies as between cities and also within a city. The proposed scheme can be regarded as fair for the following reasons:

i. It allows an option to the assessee to go by actuals if the actuals exceed the presumptive cost.
ii. It is judicially recognised that "valuation is an art, not an exact science". Any scheme that helps to bypass the notional valuation requirements and reduces the scope for litigation should be welcome.
iii. Under the existing law, the cost of properties acquired at different points of time prior to the designated date is taken uniformly at their market value determined notionally as on 1st April, 1981. This does not reflect differences arising from varying holding periods. Instead of shifting the date periodically for notional substitution of the acquisition cost, the proposed scheme permits an option to the assessee to go in for deduction on a presumptive basis at two different rates, one for assets held for more than eight years and, another for those held for less than eight years but more than three years. Keeping in view the simplification it will bring about, this classification should be regarded as reasonable.

Yet another justification for relating the deemed cost of acquisition to the sale price is that the present formula of indexation, based on the CPI is deficient in that it does not allow fully for erosion in the purchasing power embedded in monetary earnings or gains in terms of command over all categories of goods such as real property. While one may argue that the "real" gain to property owners should be computed only with reference to the price of consumer goods and services which form the CPI basket, it has to be recognised that the gain arising from the appreciation in real estate indexed only for CPI does not represent an accretion of real economic power for a house owner who sells his house property for acquiring another. The limitations of "general price level" index for inflation accounting are well known. In fact the provision for tax free roll over of certain categories of assets often allowed in the taxation of capital gains (e.g. for a residential house) derives its rationale partly from this reasoning. The scheme proposed above will go some way to take care of the deficiency of the existing formula for indexation, while simplifying the process of capital gains assessment greatly.

OVERVIEW

Direct taxes need restructuring in terms of reduced average rates and a much broader base. While the former obviously has unanimous public support, the latter is politically sensitive and prone to being ignored by Government and citizenry alike. Reductions in average rates, moreover, do not guarantee better compliance without fundamental reforms in tax administration. An attempt to broaden the tax base was made from year to year in terms of the presumptive tax on small business and trade. The revenue results are not that encouraging. Of-course, presumptive cost method in respect of long term capital gains, if introduced, may produce results which will be either dismal or encouraging. A major reason for failure of such a measure is the deep rooted fear, despite what the advertisement say, of being brought into the tax net. The fear is of higher expected future taxes, along with the apprehension of encountering the whims of tax collectors. For the Government, the lessons are quite clear. Tax collections may be poor because of the past practice of frequent hikes in tax rates. The stability of tax regime is of paramount importance. Simultaneously, there has to be a relentless drive towards better collections through incentives and threats given to tax administrators, and changes in the degree of transparency by minimising the discretionary aspects of tax laws.

As far as the equity aspects of direct taxes are concerned, too much emphasis on vertical equity through narrowing of the post-tax income differentials is often self-defeating since it encourages poor compliance. On the other hand, stress on horizontal equity in tax incidence, whereby similar income groups are taxed alike irrespective of which activity generated the income, encourages tax payment. A big gap in the horizontal equity is the absence of any significant tax on agricultural income. Understandably, there are constitutional difficulties as well as economic problems in measuring such incomes, but they are not insurmountable. A small beginning has been made in this direction. But a proper agenda is called for with a specific time frame for implementation. As far as direct taxes are concerned, the tasks are unambiguous and the mandate is clear. What is needed are a little bit of imagination and good deal of courage.

Corporate Leverage in India —A changing Scenario

Dr. G. Kotrappa*

"Neither a borrower nor a lender be" was the dictum delivered by Shakesphere through one of his epics "Merchant of Venice". But it bears no relevance today as borrowing and lending is the mainstay of modern-day economics. Not only individuals but also firms, corporate bodies and even Governments borrow. Corporate entity representing the biggest borrower next only to Government has, it appears, shifted its priority to equity source for financing its investment and other requirements during the so called 'Liberalized' period. In this write-up it is attempted to sketch the factors responsible for reduced proportion of debt capital in the total capital mobilised by companies.

The success of a corporation greatly depends upon sound financing. When the original financing has been sound, a corporation has little to fear for the future, provided it is given by a competent management.

Long term capital needs of a company arise primarily for:

a) acquiring land and buildings, plant and machinery and other fixed assets needed to setup expansion, diversification or modernization projects;
b) providing core working capital;
c) repaying previous loans; and
d) financing takeovers.

The capital necessary for above purposes may be mobilized by a company either through debt source or equity source. For a company the choice between equity and debt, in the absence of corporate income tax

* Professor, DOS in Commerce, Mysore University, M.G. Mysore - 6

and other market imperfections, is mainly governed by the difference in required rates of return between debt and equity. It may substitute debt for equity to finance its growth and other plans. However, the scope for trading on equity[1] is constrained by increase in financial risk with the rise in leverage. The enterprise continues to substitute debt for equity as long as marginal fall in overall required rate will be equal to rise in equity required rate.

However, the choice between debt and equity sources of capital for a corporate borrower is greatly influenced by the following factors:

1. Taxes on corporate income
2. Inflation
3. Controlling interest
4. Capital market reforms

TAXES

Under the existing system of taxing corporate income, debt capital produces tax deductions in the form of interest payments, a privilege equity capital is not entitled to. Because of interest deductibility, companies can lower their tax liabilities by raising the debt-equity ratio. Equity finance, therefore, represents an inferior method of fund raising. Some countries have introduced different measures to counter the bias in favour of debt financing. Mexico allows dividend deduction in the determination of corporate profits; other countries provide dividend relief at the personal income level.[2]

INFLATION

As far back as 1937, Fisher[3] theorized that nominal interest rate will be equal to real rate of interest plus the rate of inflation. If income taxes are proportional at rate T and interest payments are tax deductible, the real after tax interest rate (r) is: $r= i(1-T), \Pi$ where 'i' represents the nominal rate of interest and Π the annual expected rate of inflation. From this relationship it can be observed that a firm which enters into a contract to borrow at a fixed rate of interest benefits because of inflation. Suppose reinvestment opportunity exists for a corporate orgánisation at an expected rate of return K, investment takes place until the after-tax return K(1-T) is equal to:

$$K (1-T) = i (i-T) -\Pi$$

The implications of above mathematical relationship are illustrated in table 1. It can be observed that if rate of inflation is high, say, 8 per cent, the net cost of debt funds will be zero for T=20 per cent and it will be a net benefit of 2 per cent for T=40 per cent.

TABLE—1
Inflation, Taxes and Interest Cost

Expected Rate of Inflation (%)	Current Interest Rate (%)	Real Interest Cost (%)	After-tax Interest Cost	
			T = 20% (%)	T= 40% (%)
Nil	10	10	8	6
02	10	08	6	7
04	10	06	4	2
08	10	02	0	-2

CONTROLLING INTEREST

Perhaps one of the easiest ways of retaining controlling interest by the management of a company while financing growth is through debt capital. A great majority of our corporate entities are family owned rather than publicly owned. A study on the shareholding pattern of 519 running companies by Economic Times Research Bureau[4] has revealed that promoters/owners were firmly in control of their respective companies, with a sizable equity holding of nearly 31 per cent. A similar study[5] of 236 new companies which issued shares through prospectus during the period January 1989 to June 1991 showed that more than 37 per cent of capital was retained by the promotors in newly established companies which is significantly higher than their holdings in the older companies. Further, the desire of company managements to retain controlling interest is evident from the fact that, as Economic Times studies revealed, capital offered to the public was 28 per cent in older companies and 33 per cent in respect of new companies which continues to be much lower than stock exchange regulations norm of 60 per cent in the normal course.

CAPITAL MARKET REFORMS

The choice between debt and equity is also determined by the capital market conditions. Under a regime of tight control over capital issues, particularly with regard to fixation of premium, corporate entities are reluctant to tap equity source. The share premium provides the cushion to the issuing company required for meeting ever increasing cost of servicing equity and associated flotation cost. Throughout 1970s and 1980s, as CCI (Controller of Capital Issues) did not allow free pricing of equity capital issues, the joint stock companies were unwilling to take advantage of the vast potential demand for equity stock by the investing public.[6] The supply of equities did not keep pace with the demand for them. The companies have showed restraint in issuing equity capital.

The influencing factors discussed above were, throughout 1970s and 1980s period, in favour of debt capital prejudicing the issue of equity capital. The tax system of providing deduction of interest cost coupled with high tax incidence reduced the cost of debt capital vis-a-vis equity capital substantially. Inflation as high as 10 per cent and above during this period offered unprecedented benefits to the borrower. Besides, the CCI regulations forced corporate organizations to be sceptical about raising equity. All this resulted in high capital gearing as shown Table 2. There was an alarming shift in the debt-equity composition. While the role of equity capital as a source of long-term finance declined over the years, dependence on debt capital increased substantially with the result that capital formation was characterized by high capital gearing. The proportion of debt increased to 49 per cent during 1971-75 and further to 62 per cent during 1976-80 before reaching a peak of 65 per cent during 1986-90.

TABLE—2
Capital Gearing in Indian Corporations

Period	No.of Corporations	As % to total: Equity[1]	As % to total: Debt	Capital Gearing (%)
1961-65	304	22	28	40
1966-70	319	75	25	33
1971-75	348	51	49	98
1976-80	375	38	62	162
1981-85	1490	36	64	179
1986-90	1538	35	65	187

1. Includes preference capital
2. Ratio of debt to equity
Source: RBI Report on Currency and Finance-relevant Issues.

However, whatever premium enjoyed by corporate borrower in respect of debt capital got diluted following substantial cut in income-tax rates and reduced inflation during first half of this decade. Capital market reforms providing for free pricing of equity issues were successful in stimulating the primary market with large number of companies flooding the market with their equity issue. Consequently, debt equity mixture of corporate project finance was marked by the reversal of the trend as shown in Table–3. The capital gearing which was as high as 187 per cent during 1980s got reduced to 82 per cent during 1992-93 before increasing marginally to over 100 per cent in the following years.

TABLE—3

Debt-equity Composition during Post-liberalisation Period

Period	No.of Corporations	As % to total		Capital Gearing[2] (%)
		Equity[1]	Debt	
1992-93	426	55	45	82
1993-94	525	49	51	104
1994-95	800	45	55	122
1995-96	581	46	54	117

1. includes preference capital
2. ratio of debt to equity

Source : RBI Report on Currency and Finance-relevant issues. Pertinent Question.

The analysis of issues in the primary market reveals in similar trend as shown in Table–4. The proportion of equity component—which was less than 40 per cent upto 1991-92, increased to 63.4 per cent in 1992–93, further to 58.3 per cent in 1994-95 before reaching a peak of 74 per cent in 1994-95. However, the trend is not sustained thereafter.

TABLE—4

Debt Vs. Equity on the Primary Market

Year	Volume (Rs. Bilon)		Share (%)	
	Equity	Debt	Equity	Debt
1990-91	40.5	72.3	35.9	64.1
1991-92	57.8	87.5	39.8	60.2
1992-93	189.1	109.2	63.4	36.6
1993-94	231.1	165.0	58.3	41.7
1994-95	361.3	127.0	74.0	26.0
1995-96	181.2	92.3	66.3	33.7
1996-97 (FH)	51.4	67.6	43.2	56.8

Source : CMIE

PERTINENT QUESTION

How far this reversal of trend in corporate leverage is sustainable? The issue looms large in view of certain developments such as : (1) The Indian corporate world is under the grip of takeover fever prompting corporate managements to consolidate their controlling interest positions and to hold on equity issues to the public. (2) overall investment climate remaining subdued. The market for new capital issues failed to revive during 1996-97. During this period, the private sector companies charged even lower premium for their equity as compared to those in 1995-96. The share of premium in the total equity value fell to 23.8 per cent during 1996-97 from 41 per cent during 1995-96.[7] The proportion of equity issues in the aggregate capital issues by the non-Govt. Companies at 58.8 per cent during 1996-97 was also lower as compared with 74.5 per cent in the previous year.[8] Therefore, there is every possibility of Indian corporate sector reverting back to the regime of high capital gearing.

REFERENCES

1. Watermann, Marwin H., "*Trading on Equity*" in Wilford J. Eitman (ed.), *Essays in Business Finance, An Abror*, Mich : Masterco Press, Inc., 1963, ch.7.
2. Chad Leecher., "*Tax Policy and Tax Reform in Semi-industrial Countries*", Industry and Finance Seres, Vol. 13, World Bank, 1986.
3. Irwing Fisher "*Income in Theory and Income Taxation in Practice*", Econometrica, Jan 1937, pp l-55.
4. Economic Times, Thursday, 20th June 1991.
5. Economic Times, 25th July 1991.
6. Kotrappa G., *Corporate Taxation and Capital Formation*, Deep and Deep Pub, 1996, pp 95-97.
7. RBI Report on Currency and Finance, 1996–97.
8. RBI Report on Currency and Finance, 1996–97.

Towards Better Measure of Working Capital Performance in the Liberalised Era

Dr. (Mrs). Bishnupriya Mishra *
Dr. N.C. Kar **

Now companies are giving more emphasis on short-run as well as long-run performance in order to gain competitive advantage. The companies are trying to manage the working capital more efficiently to reap return from short-run operations also. Hence development of new parameters for measuring the working capital performance is the need of the hour. In the present study we have tried to analyse the predictive power of different financial ratios. The study is divided into two parts: Part I discusses about different liquidity measurement concepts and their limitations; Part II presents a statistical research to test the efficacy of various liquidity measures. All the companies in Automobile Industry of India have been selected as samples for the purpose of the study. The study reveals that there is a significant correlation among different financial ratios those measure profitability liquidity and cash-flows of a company. The ratios can be clubbed into different categories. The discriminant analysis with these ratios infers that cash-flow measures are better indicators than the profitability and liquidity ratios for indicating the financial health of a company. Hence the cash-flow based ratios taken together have a better predictive power than the other traditional financial ratios.

The need for working capital basically arises due to the synchronous nature of cash-flows. The cash outflows to meet the production expenses

* Faculty Member, Regional College of Management, Bhubaneshwar - 751 016

** Head, Dept. of Business Administration, Utkal University, Vanivihar, Bhubaneshwar - 751 004.

do not occur at the same time as cash proceeds from sales are realised. The longer the cash conversion cycle, the more reliance the firm has on outside financing sources. According to Accounting Principles Board of American Institute of Certified Public Accountants[1] (AICPA), "Working Capital, sometimes called net working capital is represented by the excess of current assets over current liabilities that identifies the relatively liquid portion of total enterprise capital which constitute the margin or buffer for manufacturing obligations within ordinary operating cycle of the business". One weakness of this as a measurement tool is that it combines, operating and financing decisions[2]. Joe Shulman and Raymond Co[3] suggest for breaking this traditional measure into two components: (1) working capital requirement and (2) net liquid balance. The working capital requirement consists of operating current assets minus operating current liabilities. This figure when divided by sales in rupees provides us an idea about the amount of working capital required per rupee of sales.

According to Traditional School of thinking, profitability and return are regarded as the function of long run performance whereas working capital and liquidity are regarded as a function of short run performance. But according to Modern School of thinking, competitive advantage being the key for success, the companies have to shift their emphasis to short run performance or working capital performance also. For generating return through short run operations, the companies have to concentrate their attention on working capital performance. The ability to run the company with less required working capital means the company does not have to face uncertainties and the cost of borrowing from outside sources becomes less. The smaller the working capital requirement to sales ratio, the shorter the cash cycle will be, resulting in more financial flexibility for the firm. Hence it is necessary to develop new parameters to examine working capital performance. We have tried to identify the liquidity measures that have a greater predictive ability than other measures. Our study is divided into two parts; part one discusses about different liquidity measurement concepts and their limitations; part two presents a statistical research to test the efficacy of the various liquidity measures.

PART—I

CONCEPT OF LIQUIDITY

There are two approaches to liquidity measurement:

1. Quantitative Approach
2. Qualitative Approach

The Quantitative Approach

The quantitative approach (early 19th century) is basically a stock concept. Liquidity is defined as the quantum of "near cash assets" available with the firm to meet its day-to-day requirements. The higher the quantum of such assets, the higher liquidity the firm possesses. By near cash assets is meant the assets which can be converted into cash within a short period.

As is obvious, this is stock concept. Hence the position of a firm at one point of time is revealed by this measure and not its ability to generate cash. There is a possibility of confusion regarding the near cash assets. Which assets can be converted into cash and at what prices is a moot point. The current assets "get converted" into cash in the course of business and not that the firm can readily convert them into cash as and when it so desires. Hence they do not measure liquidity.

The Qualitative Approach

This approach defines liquidity as the ability of the firm to generate cash (either by selling assets or by making liabilities) to meet potential expenses both in the short and the long term. In the qualitative sense, liquidity is specific, objective and limited in its purview. In the quantitative approach, liquidity management covers structure and utilisation of cash and its receivables, whereas in the qualitative approach, liquidity explores all possible means of raising sources and utilising them in a way to meet all obligations in the best manner.

The approaches to measure liquidity has been developed in three phases:

THE FIRST PHASE

The degree of liquidity was considered to be a function of net working capital. This was basically the quantitative approach to measure liquidity. This being an absolute measure, comparison between firms was a problem. Hence, the concept of ratios to measure liquidity was developed. Some of these include current ratio, quick ratio and supporting ratios.

Conventionally it was belived that current ratio of 2:1 or more was indicative of a fairly liquid position. However, later on the industry average ratio was used to compare the liquidity position of a firm. As long as this value was close to the industry average, it was considered a satisfactory position. Under quick ratio, stock, being the most undependable source as regards its value and time of conversion, was deducted from current assets and compared with current liabilities. A conventional norm of 1:1 was considered good. The above two measures were used as a first time test of liquidity and some supporting ratios like inventory turnover, average collection period, creditors' turnover, cash position ratio etc. were used to portray the full picture of the firm.

The criticism to these ratios as a measure of liquidity are as follows:

1. This is again a 'stock' view. This has been explained while describing the quantitative approach.
2. The current assets as such are not a measure of liquidity as current assets 'get' converted into cash in due course of time and not that the firm 'can' convert them into cash at any point of time.
3. It was found that the ratios vary over time and a tendency to fix them (such as 2:1 for current ratio) may be detrimental for the firm.
4. The efficacy of the ratio is an indicator of liquidity. Researchers have found that these ratios have failed to predict the sickness of firms.

THE SECOND PHASE

In this phase, the move was from stock concept to flow concept of measuring liquidity. Some of the important ratios used were:

1. Bierman's Measure
2. Interval Measures
3. Liquidity Flow Index

All these measures tried to combine the stock measures with flow measures. However the limitations of these measures were that they could be used for very specific and limited conditions.

THE THIRD PHASE

This phase represents the latest developments in measuring liquidity and were developed in late 70's and early 80's. The measure are cashflow ratios, significant balance sheet ratios and cashflow index.

1. Cash Flow Ratios

* CFO/Total Debt
* CFO/Total Assets
* CFO/Capital Employed

Where CFO= Cash From Operations

2. Significant balance sheet ratios

This measure was given by Robertson[4] He constructed a model consisting of 5 ratios for measuring overall financial health, which included 3 liquidity measures as given below:

* (Current Assets—Total Debt) /Current Liabilities
* (Equity—Total Debt) /Total Debt
* (Liquid Assets—Bank Overdraft) /Creditors

3. Cash Flow Index

This was suggested by Parasar[5]. He developed a framework for measuring liquidity using 4 basic cash flow indices and 3 summary indices. The cash flow indices are:

* Priority cash outflow index
* Discretionary cash outflow index
* Operational cash outflow index
* Financial cash outflow index

The summary indices are developed by combining the basic indices and are as follows:

* Operational liquidity index
* Financial liquidity index
* Company's liquidity index

PART—II

SAMPLE SELECTION

We have selected the Automobile industry for the purpose of the study. The data for the year 1995-96 have been analysed. All the companies in this industry are included for analysis. (Appendix I)

RATIOS IDENTIFIED

We have selected the following sets of ratios:

Profitability ratios

(PBDIT/TA) Return on Assets
(PBDIT)CE) Return on Capital Employed

We took profits before interest and depreciation in these ratios as we are interested in the operating efficiency of the firms.

Traditional Liquidity ratios

(CR) Current Ratio = CA/CL
(QR) Quick Ratio = (CA-Inventory)/CL

These are traditional measures of liquidity which dominated the first phase of thinking about liquidity measures.

Cash flow based ratios

(CFO/S) Cash Flow from Operations/Sales
(CFO/TA) Cash Flow from Operations/Total Assets
(CFO/D) Cash Flow from Operations/Debt

These ratios have dominated the current thinking about liquidity measures and form a part of phase three.

OBJECTIVE OF THE STUDY

We have tried to study:

1. Whether the ratios be clubbed into the three categories as shown above; and
2. Which of the above categories of ratio is a better indicator of the financial health of the company?

HYPOTHESES

We have tested two hypotheses to fulfil the objective of our study.

Hypothesis—1

Null Hypothesis

$H_0$1: There is no significant correlation among the above ratios and the ratios cannot be clubbed into separate categories.

Alternative Hypothesis:

$H_1$1: There is a significant correlation among the above ratios and the ratios can be clubbed into separate categories.

Hypothesis—2

Null Hypothesis

$H_0$2: Cash flow measures are not better indicators of health of a company.

Alternative Hypothesis:

$H_1$2: Cash flow measures are better indicators of health of a company.

METHODOLOGY TO TEST HYPOTHESIS NO.1

* We conducted Factor analysis with all the ratios as the variables for the 28 sample companies.
* The factors were examined to club the ratios into groups.

Findings

* Factor analysis gave us three factors. The factors with the variables are: (Appendix II may be referred)
  Factor—PBDIT/TA (0.84512), PBDIT/CE (0.88009)
  Factor 2—CR (0.87244), QR (0.92939)
  Factor 3—CFO/S (0.93226), CFO/TA (0.64856), CFO/D (0.52311)
* The correlation between the factors are:

	FACTOR 1	FACTOR 2	FACTOR 3
Factor 1	0.82222	-0.56021	0.10064
Factor 2	0.56914	0.80735	-0.15578
Factor 3	0.00602	0.18536	0.98265

* From the analysis we see that the ratios have been grouped into three distinct factors based on the high correlation.

Inference

$H_0 1$ is rejected. The above ratios can be grouped into three categories:

Factor 1—Profitability Ratios
Factor 2—Traditional Ratios
Factor 3—Cash Flow Based ratios

METHODOLOGY TO TEST HYPOTHESIS NO. 2

* Assuming that the profitability ratios are good indicators for classifying companies we have grouped the 28 companies into two categories.
  Group 1: ROCE > Industry Average (The "good" companies)
  Group 0: ROCE < Industry Average (The "bad" companies)
* To check the predictive power of the traditional ratios we conducted a discriminant analysis with these ratios.
* A similar discriminant analysis was done with the cash flow based ratios.
* The classification statistics was used to see which of the two sets is a better discriminator.

Findings

* For the traditional ratios the statistics are as follows: (Appendix III may be referred)

Eigen value	0.1202
Correlation	0.3276
Wilks Lambda	0.8927
Groups correctly classified	64.29%

* For the cash flow based ratios the statistics are:

Eigen value	0.3001
Correlation	0.4805
Wilks Lambda	0.7692
Groups correctly classified	71.43%

* From the analysis we see that the cash flow based ratios classify the companies better than the traditional ratios.

Inference

$H_0 2$ is rejected. Cash flow based ratios are a better indicator of the financial health of a company.

LIMITATION

* The sample size for the study was small, hence thorough test for statistical significance could not be done.
* Further, the analysis was done for the year 1995-96 only. A time series analysis over 3-5 years would have given a better trend.

CONCLUSION

The study reveals that there is a significant correlation among different financial ratios those measure profitability, liquidity and cash-flows of a company. The ratios can be clubbed into different categories. The discriminant analysis with these ratios infers that cash-flow measures are better indicators than the profitability and liquidity ratios for indicating the financial health of a company. Hence the cash-flow based ratios taken together have a better predictive power than the other traditional financial ratios.

REFERENCES

1. Accounting Principles Board, "*Concepts and Objectives of Financial Statements*" AICPA, New York, Nov. 1978.

2. Maness, T.S., "*The Cash-Flow Time Line and the Credit Manager*", Business Credit, July-Aug, 1994, p.11.

3. Shulman, J.M. and Cox, R.A.K., "*An Integrative Approach to Working Capital Management*", Journal of Cash Management, Vol. 5 (No.6), 1985, pp. 64-70.

4. Robertson. J., "*A Ratio Model to Measure Changes in Financial Health*", Management Accounting (U.K.), April, 1985.

5. Parasar, S.P., "*A New Look at Corporate Liquidity*", Indian Management, May 1984, p. 25.

APPENDIX 1

Sl. No.	Companies	PBDIT/TA	PBDIT/CE	CFO/S	CFO/TA	CFO/D	QR	CR	GRP
1	2	3	4	5	6	7	8	9	10
1.	Ashok Leyland	13.14	18.11	-6.80	-6.47	-0.16	0.52	2.17	0
2.	Atlas-Cycle Ind.	11.59	21.85	0.17	0.47	0.01	0.91	1.51	0
3.	Bajaj Auto	36.87	46.80	19.82	30.06	2.66	0.72	1.64	1
4.	Bajaj Tempo	32.54	75.52	3.15	6.62	0.41	0.07	1.17	1
5.	Daewoo Motors India Ltd.	10.78	72.10	8.63	6.53	9.28	-0.26	0.69	1
6.	Eicher Ltd.	25.39	40.03	6.66	19.60	0.39	0.38	1.41	1
7.	Eicher Motor Ltd.	17.74	38.32	7.24	13.80	0.43	0.56	1.35	0
8.	Elgi Equipments	20.88	35.14	11.83	17.73	0.39	0.74	1.51	0
9.	Greaves Ltd.	13.95	25.43	5.03	6.88	0.20	0.66	1.50	0
10.	Hero Honda Motors Ltd.	24.63	55.15	8.11	21.19	1.04	0.38	1.00	1
11.	Hindustan Motors Ltd.	17.01	29.70	5.59	9.69	0.47	1.36	8.97	0
12.	Kinetic Engineering Ltd.	24.27	38.24	12.72	23.18	0.83	0.25	1.29	0
13.	Kinetic Honda Motor Ltd.	13.50	27.28	-3.70	-13.67	-0.53	0.27	1.26	0
14.	LML Ltd.	20.72	66.21	6.94	12.70	0.40	0.32	1.07	1
15.	Maharashtra Scooters Ltd.	17.30	25.59	4.12	6.60	1.84	0.46	1.19	0
16.	Mahindra & Mahindra Ltd.	22.23	36.66	13.55	22.33	1.00	0.26	0.97	0

{Cont.}.......

1	2	3	4	5	6	7	8	9	10
17.	Majestic Auto Ltd.	10.23	20.06	9.82	13.87	0.30	0.35	0.94	0
18.	Maruti Udyog Ltd.	26.65	78.02	0.00	0.00	0.00	0.47	0.99	1
19.	Pal-Peugeot Ltd.			12.08	-13.16	0.26	0.44	0.97	0
20.	Premier Automobiles Ltd.	11.25	59.79	44.42	43.68	4.19	0.33	0.84	1
21.	Scooters India Ltd.	1.05	-0.11	-99.95	-187.58	-0.49	0.03	0.09	0
22.	Sooraj Automobiles Ltd.	6.01	10.68	0.00	0.00	0.00	0.74	1.42	0
23.	Sunku Auto Ltd.	35.85	45.52	0.97	1.13	0.13	0.52	2.34	1
24.	Swaraj Mazda Ltd.	10.92	60.78	-1.16	-2.36	-0.07	0.28	1.19	1
25.	TVS-Suzuki Ltd.	38.88	86.75	13.18	42.36	2.45	0.19	0.96	1
26.	Tata Engineering & Loco	22.65	44.61	12.32	19.42	0.75	0.49	1.06	1
27.	Vespa Car Co. Ltd.	-0.66	0.60	385.71	1.99	0.02	0.01	0.11	0
28.	Whirlpool India Ltd.	-2.66	-3.73	-17.65	-25.33	-1.75	1.84	4.00	0
	Mean	17.89	39.08	16.53	2.54	0.87	0.47	1.56	
	Std. Deviation	10.73	24.04	74.47	39.66	1.95	0.40	1.59	

APPENDIX II

FACTOR ANALYSIS

Final Statistics

Variables	Communality	Factor	Eigen value	% of variance	Cumulative %
PBDIT/TA	0.74678	1	2.59734	37.1	37.1
PBDIT/CE	0.87230	2	1.72379	24.6	61.7
NCFO/S	0.91630	3	1.21133	17.3	79.0
NCFO/TA	0.87726				
NCFO/D	0.45793				
QR	0.89659				
CR	0.76530				

Rotated Factor Matrix

	FACTOR 1	FACTOR 2	FACTOR 3
PBDIT/TA	0.84512	0.01332	-0.17995
PBDIT/CE	0.88009	-0.28681	-0.12445
NCFD/S	-0.14648	-0.16046	0.93226
NCFD/TA	0.52881	0.21253	0.64856
NCFD/D	0.49061	-0.44952	0.52311
QR	-0.17321	0.92939	-0.05314
CR	0.07741	0.87244	-0.04373

Factor Transformation Matrix

	FACTOR 1	FACTOR 2	FACTOR 3
Factor 1	0.82222	-0.56021	0.10064
Factor 2	0.56914	0.80735	-0.15578
Factor 3	0.00602	0.18536	0.98265

APPENDIX III

DISCRIMINANT ANALYSIS OF TRADITIONAL RATIOS

Group Means	QR	CR
Group 0	0.58750	1.82813
Group 1	0.32417	1.19667
Total	0.47464	1.55750

Canonical Discriminant Functions

Fcn	Eigen Value	% of Variance	Cum. %	Canonical Correlation		Fcn	Wilks Lambda	Chisquare	DF	Sig.
1	0.1202	100.00	100.00	0.3276	:	0	0.8927	2.8380	2	0.2419

Standardized Canonical Discriminant Function Coefficients

	Func 1
QR	1.14834
CR	.22975

Canonical Discriminant Functions evaluated at Group Means (Group Centroids)

Group	Func 1
0	0.28936
1	-0.38582

Classification Results

Actual Group		No. of cases	Predicted Group Membership 0	Predicted Group Membership 1
Group	0	16	10 (62.5%)	6 (37.5%)
Group	1	12	4 (33.3%)	8 (66.7%)

Per cent of "grouped" cases correctly classified : 64.29%

DISCRIMINANT ANALYSIS OF CASH FLOW BASED RATIOS

Group Means	CFO/S	CFO/TA	CFO/D
Group 0	21.23500	-8.10438	0.17625
Group 1	10.25333	16.74417	1.80250
Total	16.52857	2.54500	0.87321

Canonical Discriminant Functions

Fcn	Eigen Value	% of Variance	Cum%	Canonical Correlation		Fcn	Wilks Lambda	Chisquare	DF	Sig
1	0.3001	100.00	100.00	0.4805	:	0	0.7692	6.4300	3	0.0925

Standardized Canonical Discriminant Function Coefficients

	Func 1
CFO/S	-0.36741
CFO/TA	0.57442
CFO/D	0.73845

Canonical Discriminant Functions evaluated at Group Means (Group Centroids)

Group	Func 1
0	-0.45718
1	0.60957

Classification Results

Actual Group		No. of cases	Predicted Group Membership 0	Predicted Group Membership 1
Group	0	16	13 (81.3%)	3 (18.8%)
Group	1	12	5 (41.7%)	7 (58.3%)

Per cent of 'grouped' cases correctly classified : 71.43%

Multinationals Finance —Some Issues

Dr. S.P. Saha*

INTRODUCTION

You are certainly familiar with business already because it is all around you everyday. Challenge after challenge has confronted business in recent years. These challenges have produced several noticeable trends in the business world. Business has become more socially responsible its impact of international society of a business decision is now weighed in most management decision making. Business has become more conscious of its operating costs. Business has found new markets abroad but has encountered increasing competition from foreign producers at home.

The Indian business sector presents a mix picture. Private enterprise has proved to be very effective economic system for Indian business scenario through multinational corporations (MNCs). MNCs have provided a high degree of economic freedom, a low cost of living, substantial product choice, high earnings, considerable public welfare and many other economic benefits. India is becoming a more prosperous nation because of the entry of the private enterprise system after economic liberalisation. Since then in our economy, one may find dozen of giant MNCs, operating under vary conditions like 100 per cent owned subsidiaries, majority companies, minority companies, licences, technical collaboration agreements with or without equity participation in the companies.

* Lecturer and Head, Deptt. of Commerce, SMDP Mahila College, Madhubani (Bihar), L.N. Mithila University, Darbhanga.

A firm that operates in two or more nations is defined as a multinational corporation. Such a company has a base corporation in one country (the parent company) and operates branches and subsidiaries throughout the world. Its share are normally owned mostly, if not entirely by the residents of the parent company's country. Multinational Corporations are also termed today as the global gaints because the political boundaries of the nation states become to narrow and constrained to provide adequate scope for the large scale operations of these enterprises and this is why they have been spreading in the world with substantial freedom of producing and selling their products in a host of national markets and begetting corporate offspring of various nationalities in unlimited numbers.

FINANCING TO MNC

The long term strategy for combating the multidimensional challenges of the multinational companies has to be created within the parameter of financial management. In the changed economic milieu of multinational corporations, the importance of financial management for them have greatly increased. India's multinational will have to draw up their futuristic vision by way of sound financial management. Through proper corporate finance, the multinationals have to visualise how much capital desire to invest in and where the primary need of multinational finance has to be invested.

Within the framework of overall corporate finance, the multinationals have to develop long term and short-term financial management. However, in the changed environment the immediate need of finance of a multinational firm has to be survival for which emphasis will have to be placed a balanced inter-relationship between long and short-term uses and sources of funds. The engines that are driving the multinational firms are financial management. The financial management of the multinational firms should be to achieve international competitiveness in the field of finance. This is in keeping with the very logic of finance itself. Any individual unit/organisation of finance has the power within it to grow, expand and become a multinational finance. The history of any MNCs bears this out. The history of the MNCs also bears out the fact that an MNC can originate in any nation. However, in the discourse on multinational finance, it is always assumed that an MNC in a western animal. However, this in far from correct and among the most dynamic multinational companies present today the Asian Multinationals also have their pride of place. Moreover, the latter's presence can be witnessed in the most advanced sectors of global production.

Another implicit assumption as regards the MNC is that financial source from west to east. However, the reverse is also true. To give a few examples, Hyundai, the Korean multinational is setting up a one billion pound semi-conductor plant in Scotland. The second phase of source of fund is understood to being into Scotland another 1.4 billion pounds. There are presently more than twenty multinational companies of Korea manufacturing in Britain, apart from the fact that large Korean investments were around 30 million pounds, in 1995 the total investments including that of Hyundai and its rival Samsung Corporation and LG Group total 3.16 billion pounds. Another Korean multinational Daewoo has invested 1.5 billion dollars (in the process buging up a leading French Company) in france to make electronic parts.

On the basis of forging example, the study of multinational finance takes traditional managerial finance as its starting point, then builds on the models of capital budgeting, cost of capital and working capital management. However, multinational financial management must also take into account international differences in financial markets and institutions. Accordingly, multinational firms have to take into account these following aspects in view of their financial management separately—

(1) Foreign exchange rate and international monetary system,
(2) Procedures for analyzing foreign investment, and
(3) The financial management of foreign assets.

FOREIGN EXCHANGE RATE AND INTERNATIONAL MONETARY SYSTEM

All exchange rate designates the number of units of one currency that can be exchanged for another. The exchange rates, or the number of Indian rupees required to buy one unit of currency. For the twelve leading trading partners of India appear in the Economic Time daily. See, for example, the rates given on June 20, 1996 as shown in the Table :

	Indian rupees required to buy one unit of foreign currency	Number of units of foreign currency per Indian Rs.
British Pound Sterling	65.2500	0.01532
US Dollar	38.2000	0.02618
Canadian Dollar	25.4800	0.03924
Deutsche Mark	20.6800	0.04835
Dutch Guilder	17.2200	0.05807
Swiss Franc	26.1500	0.03824
French Franc	6.0000	0.16666
Swedish Krona	4.6000	0.21739
Italian Lira	0.0210	47.61904
Japanese Yen	0.2700	3.70371
Australian Dollar	21.3200	0.04491
Saudi Riyal	10.3000	0.09708

Source—The Economic Times.

From the end of World War II until 1971, the world was on a fixed exchange rate system, administered by the International Monetary Fund. Under this system, the US Dollar was the base currency used to establish the relative values of all other major currencies and exchange rates between other currencies and exchange rates between other currencies and the Dollar were controlled within narrow limits. For example, in 1971 the Indian Rupee was fixed at 7.50 Rupees per Dollar.

Fluctuations occurred because of third devaluation of rupees. The current Account position of India faced serious pressure simultaneously on various fronts. Between October, 1990 and March, 1991 the real effective exchange rate of the rupee appreciated by 2 per cent, as a result of widening inflation differentials between India and the major industrialised countries. The Nominal effective exchange Rate (NEER) is a weighted average of the bilateral nominal exchange Rate of rupee against the foreign currencies. The real Effective Exchange Rate is NEER adjusted for prize differentials among multinational firms. All this had resulted in an erosion of India's multinational firms with other countries regarding international competitiveness.

With the approval of the IMF, a country could devalue its currency if it experienced difficulty over a long period in preventing its exchange rate from falling below the lower limit, and if it was running out of the gold and other currencies necessary to buy its own currency and thus prop up its price. For just these reasons, the Indian rupee was revalued in 1994. In talking of the impact of the exchange rate changes, one must reckon with legs in the response to exchange rate changes. However, in the present context, the inflow of foreign collaboration through MNCs or their subsidiaries donot imply subjugation. The share of India in direct foreign investment when compared with China, Brazil, Mexico etc. is very low. Devaluation of rupee or poor exchange rate can also be effected with more investment being made by other economically developed MNCs.

FLOATING EXCHANGE RATE

Devaluation and revaluations occurred only rarely before 1971. They were usually accompanied by severe international financial repercussions, partly because nations tended to postpone these needed measures until economic pressures had built up to explosive proportions. For this and other reasons, the old international monetary system came to a dramatic close in 1971. When the US Dollar, the foundation upon which all other currencies were anchored, was allowed to flood.

Under a system of floating exchange rates, currency prices are allowed to seek their own levels without much governmental intervention. The present world monetary system is known as a managed floating system : Major world currency rates float with market forces, unrestricted by any internationally agreed-upon limits. However, Central Ban of each country does intervene in the foreign exchange market, buying and selling its currency to smooth out exchange rate fluctuations to some extent. Each Central Bank also tries to keep its average exchange rate at a level deemed desirable by its governments economic policy. This is important, because exchange rates have a profound effect on the level of import and exports, which is turn influence the level of domestic employment.

After that, between June and July 1991 third devaluation took place, by which the rupee value was decreased by 20 per cent in terms of selected basket of currencies consequently, the value of hard currencies increased as following:

Currencies	June, 28,1991	July, 1,1991	July, 3,1991	Percentage change
1. Dollar	21.14	23.14	25.95	23.07
2. Sterling Pound	34.36	37.47	41.59	21.04
3. Deutsche Mark	11.75	12.80	14.15	20.78
4. Yen	15.31	16.86	18.68	23.33
5. Swiss Franc	13.60	14.93	16.14	23.12
6. French Franc	03.47	03.78	04.18	20.55
7. Lira	15.77	17.24	18.89	20.02

Above table shows how Dollar, British Pound, Deutsche Mark, Japanese Yen, Swiss Franc, French Franc and Italy's Lira moved in comparison to the rupee from Jun 28, 1991 to July 3, 1991. The exchange rate in percentage is high of Dollar and Yen showing 23.07 and 23.33 respectively. The Pound, the Franc and the Lira, on the other hand, indicate a same exchange rate of changing. The root cause of these divergent trends was the relative strengths of the British, German, American, Japanese and other developed economies versus that of the Indian economy, and the relative inflation rates in all seven countries.

TRADING IN FOREIGN EXCHANGE

Importers, exporters, and tourists, as well as governments, buy and sell currencies in the foreign exchange market. In India, Interbank Foreign Exchange (FOREX) is established where the transactions of international trade occur. For example, an Indian trader imports automobiles from U.S.A., payment will probably be made in U.S.A. Dollar. The importer buys Dollars through FOREX in the foreign exchange market, much as one buys common stocks on the Bombay Stock Exchange or the National Stock Exchange. However, while stock and commodity exchanges have organised trading floors, the foreign exchange market consists of a network of brokers and banks based in Bombay, New York , London, Tokyo and other financial centres. Most buy and sell orders are conducted by cablegram and telephone.

PROCEDURES FOR ANALYZING POTENTIAL FOREIGN INVESTMENTS

Although the same basic principles of investment analysis apply in both foreign and domestic operations, there are some key differences. First, the cash flow analysis is much more complex for overseas investments. Most multinational firms set up a separate subsidiary in which they operate. The relevant cash flows are the dividends and royalties repatriated by each subsidiary to the parent company. These cash flows must be converted to the currency of the parent company and thus are subject to future exchange rate changes.

Dividends and royalties are normally taxed by both foreign and domestic governments. Furthermore, a foreign government may restrict the amount and nature of cash flows that may be repatriated to the parent company. For example, some governments place a ceiling (a percentage of the company's net worth) on the amount of cash dividends that may be paid by a subsidiary to its parent company. Such restrictions are normally intended to force multinational firms to reinvest their earnings in the foreign country, although they are sometimes imposed to prevent large currency outflows which might destabilize exchange rate. Finally, depreciation cash flows of the subsidiary are usually not directly available to the parent company, since they are not part of earnings from which dividends are paid.

In addition to the complexities of the cash flow analysis, the cost of capital is generally higher for a foreign project than for an excivalent domestic project because foreign projects are generally riskier. This higher risk arises from two primary sources : (1) Exchange risk and (2) Sovereign risk.

Exchange risk refers to the fact that exchange rate fluctuations. This increases the inherent uncertainty about cash flows to the parent. In other words, foreign projects have an added risk element relating to what the basic cash flows will be worth in the parent's home currency.

Sovereign risk refers both to the possibility of expropriation and to an unanticipated restrictions on cash flows to the parent company, such as higher controls on repatriation of dividends or higher taxes. For example the risk of expropriation of The United States assets abroad is small in traditionally friendly and stable countries such as Britain or Switzerland. However, in the East European countries and in most parts of the developing world of Latin America, Africa, the Far East and Asia, the risk may be substantial. Following table shows the amount of expropriated

US sets from 1917 to 1995 in various parts of the world. Expropriations since the table was compiled including those of American-based companies in India after liberalisation.

EXPROPRIATIONS OF US ASSETS BY FOREIGN GOVERNMENTS

Country	Year	Funds Cost (in millions)
USSR	1917-20	$ 175
Mexico	1938	120
East Europe	1945-48	240
Cuba	1959-60	1400
Argentina	1963	237
Indonesia	1965	160
India	1995	191

Source : 'The Expropriation of American Companies', Business World Jan. 1996, p.-41.

CAPITAL BUDGETING FOR MULTINATIONAL

Capital budgeting in similar in principle to security valuation future cash flows as estimated, risks are appraised and reflected in a cost of capital discount rate, all cash flows are put on a present value basis and, if a project net present value is positive, it is accepted. In the same way, the principles of capital budgeting in a multinational setting can be illustrated Cipla Ltd's analysis of a proposed plant in Colombo, Sri Lanka with the CSIR to establish a laboratory in view of manufacturing a new molecule for the treatment of diabetes. Cipla has become India-based first multinational firm in the field of pharmaceuticals. If the plant is built, a new subsidiary will be incorporated in Sri Lanka. will be financed only with common stock, all of which will be owned by the parent company.

The cost of capital used to analyse the plant is 15 per cent. Sri Lanka has a 20 per cent corporate income tax, and there is no withholding tax on dividend paid.

While there is no restriction on dividend repatriation, depreciation cash flows may not be repatriated except when the company is liquidated. The investment, to be made in January 1991, consists almost entirely of plant and equipment, and the cost will be 50 million Sri Lankan rupees. Because of the thin population of this country, demand of pharmaceutical products and the Sri Lankan market, Cipla expects to own the company for only five years. At the end of the five years (in 1995), it will sell the fixed assets of the company for an estimated 125 million Sri Lankan rupees. Following table summarizes the projected income statements:

PROJECTED CASH FLOWS FOR 1991-95 (MILLION OF SR)

Particulars	1991	1992	1993	1994	1995
Revenue or net sales	50.00	55.00	60.00	65.00	70.00
Operating cost	30.00	30.00	35.00	35.00	40.00
Depreciation	5.00	5.00	5.00	5.00	5.00
Income	15.00	20.00	20.00	25.00	25.00
Corporate Tax	3.00	4.00	4.00	5.00	5.00
Net Income	12.00	16.00	16.00	20.00	20.00
Dividend Repatriated	12.00	16.00	16.00	20.00	20.00
India Tax	4.50	6.00	6.00	7.50	7.50
After Tax Dividend	7.5	10.00	10.00	12.50	12.50

Since the cash flows from depreciation cannot be repatriated until the company is liquidated at the end of 1995, they will be invested in Sri Lankan government bonds to each after-tax interest at the rate of 8 per cent. The accumulated and interest compounded depreciation cash flows at the termination of the project is shown in following table:

DEPRECIATION CASH FLOWS

Year of Depreciation	Amount (millions of SR)	Future value Interest factor at 8 per cent	Terminal value in 1995 (millions of SR)
1991	5.00	1.3605	6.802
1992	5.00	1.2597	6.299
1993	5.00	1.1664	5.832
1994	5.00	1.0800	5.400
1995	5.00	1.0000	5.000
		Total	29.333

The next step in the analysis are :·(1) to convert the annual cash flows from SRs to IRs and (2) to find the net present value of the project. These steps are shown below in a tabular form.

CASH FLOWS TO PARENT COMPANY (CIPLA) AND PATIENT'S NET PRESENT VALUE

Year	Cash flows (millions) of SR)	Exchange rate	Cash Flows (million of IR)	PV/F 15 per cent	PV of Cash flows million of IR)
	(1)	(2)	(3)	(4)	(5)
1991	07.500	1.40	5.357	0.8696	4.658
1992	10.000	1.42	7.042	0.7561	5.324
1993	10.000	1.48	6.756	0.6575	4.442
1994	12.500	1.50	8.333	0.5718	4.764
1995	66.833	1.52	43.969	0.4972	21.861
				IR	41.049
Less, initial investment of 50 million SR at 1.52 SR per IR					32.894
Net present value of project IR					08.155 (in million)

Column 1 of above table gives the annual Cash flows in SRs. From 1991 to 1994, dividends represent the only cash flow, but in 1995 cash flow of 66.833 million SRs consists of dividends (12.5 million SRs), the estimated sale price of the fixed assets (25 million SRs), and the interest accumulated depreciation cash flows (29.333 million SRs).

The estimated exchange rates are shows in column 2. The current rate, 1.40 SRs to the one Indian Rupee is expected to hold during 1991, but the SR is expected to depreciate thereafter at the rate of 1.42, 1.48, 1.50 and 1.52 respectively in succeeding year.

Dividing the cash flows in SRs (column 1) by the exchange rates (column 2) gives the expected cash flows in Indian Rupees as shown in column 3. The IR cash flows are converted to present value basis in column 5, and the sum of the annual PV cash flows is Rs. 41.049 million. By substracting the initial cost of the project, Rs. 32.894 million, from the PV of the inflows. We obtain the project's NPV Rs. 8.155 million. Since it is positive, the project should be accepted.

SOURCES OF FUNDS FOR FOREIGN INVESTMENT

In the preceding example, we assumed that the Foreign Subsidiary obtains all of its capital as common equity supplied by the parent. Several other sources of funds exist including (i) sale of common stock to local residents, (ii) borrowing from local residents, and (iii) borrowing in the world financial markets.

Selling common stock to residents of foreign countries has both good and bad features. It can result in loss of control of the subsidiary if the parent company owns less than fifty per cent of its shares. Some countries require majority ownership by local residents. This allows the country to have some control over major decisions made by corporations operating within its boundaries, and it also enables the country to retain part of the company's profits. However, this is not necessarily bad from the point of view of the multinational corporation—local participation may be a desirable feature in countries with less stable governments since it provides an incentive for the local residents to exert pressure against the threat of expropriation or other interference. Similar protection is obtained by borrowing funds in the subsidiary's country. If the subsidiary company is highly leveraged, using debt from local sources, expropriation will result in only minimal losses to parent.

Large number of multinational corporations, especially those operating in India and other developing countries, make extensive use of US Dollar. While multinational firms, operating in European countries, do their transactions through Euro Dollar. A Curo Dollar is a deposit of United States Dollar held in a European bank. Since the US Dollar is strong and relatively strong, many multinational corporations belonging to developed economy conduct transactions in US Dollar and they use the Euro Dollar market for long term loans and a short-term repository for excess funds.

For a developing economy like India, MNC is an expensive bargain from foreign investments point of view. These days, when developing countries are struggling with massive foreign debt, and their struggling with massive foreign debt, and their development plans are hold up due to paucity of fund. This may be considered as a serious drawback. Companies in India generally marketed through western multinationals do not contribute much foreign exchange in their original investment, there is no restriction on them to send back profit in foreign exchange. This creates problems for national economy.

MANAGEMENT OF FOREIGN ASSETS

The long term strategy for combating the multidimensional challenges of the multinational has to be crafted within the parameter of managing the foreign assets. Once decisions for managing foreign assets are laid down then the question arises how best to use them. This involves knowing how can fluctuating exchange rates be adjusted with local currencies. On Dec. 8, 1996 The Business World Journal reported that the Cipla Ltd. was losing Rs. 3,00,000 in earnings every month, alongwith the Sri Lankan rupees moved up one per cent against the Indian rupee. This happened because this Corporate Organisation's Sri Lankan subsidiary had about SRs 67.9 million worth of debt denominated in SR. Since the interest and principal on the debt had to be paid in SR, a one per cent appreciation of the SR meant in terms of IR, the company had to pay more IRs to pay the SRs needed to service the debt. For example, the average exchange rate of SR for IR was IR 0.841 per SR in Nov. 1996 but it had appreciated to IR 0.871 per by December, 1996. The debt amount of Cipla Ltd. in SRs would therefore appear as follows:

Month	SR/IR	Debt in SR	Debt in IR
November'96	0.841	80,824,800	6,79,73,656
December'96	0.871	80,824,800	7,03,98,400
Increase in IRs value of debt		Rs.	24,24,744

On the basis of the above-mentioned example, it is stated that the increase in the IR equivalent of, foreign debt is reported as an income loss. Such a loss is known, as a transaction loss. Since it arises from 'translating' financial statements from a foreign currency to Indian Rupee.

Had Cipla Ltd. owned current assets denominated in SR, its position would have been reversed : an appreciation would have led to losses. Had Cipla Ltd. held both current assets and owed money denominated in SR, then the difference between these two items would be its net monetary position. The net position indicates whether or not the Company has a net translation gain or loss. Therefore, multinational corporations have devised a number of ways to minimise the likelihood of trnaslation losses.

FOREIGN EXCHANGE EXPOSURE

An exposure to losses due to changing exchange rates is called foreign exchange exposure. It exists whenever the amount of assets and liabilities denominated in each foreign currency are not exact balance Monetary instruments like Cipla Ltd.'s debt are obviously exposed, as are monetary assets such as held as SR. Non-monetary assets can also be exposed.

If a multinational firm's income is to be reported properly to investors, the effects of changes in the value of assets and liabilities must be analysed properly. But, since it is extremely difficult to determine the effects of changes in currency values on assets.

Before Financial Accounting Standards Board was introduced in 1976, multinational Corporations accounted for their translation gains and losses in a variety of laws, often in the manner that best helped them present a good profit picture. In the way of financing the MNCs, IASB has standardised accounting practices as follows :

(1) All current assets and liabilities must be translated at the exchange rates prevailing at the end of each quarter.
(2) All inventories must be translated at historic rates; that is, they must be valued at the rates in effect when the goods were placed in inventory rather than at current rates.

Hedging Exposures

Many multinational Corporations complain that reporting translation gains and losses in this manner their earnings volatile and subject to the vagaries of exchange rate fluctuations. Exchange rates may rise one quarter, then fall the next under such circumstances, the duty of financial manager of multinational Corporations becomes foremost. What actions can be taken to reduce the foreign exchange exposure. This is known as hedging exposure. Consider our precious example of Cipla Ltd.'s debt of 80.2 million SRs. If the financial manager fears an appreciation of the SR, all of Cipla Ltd.'s Sri Lankan debt could be retired and replaced by borrowing in IR, other in SAARC market or financial institutions or FOREX in India. However, this would be desirable only if IRs funds are available at acceptable interest rates. Alternatively, the financial manager could use *forward contracts* in the locals foreign exchange market. SR can be bought for IR for current value or they can be bought at some future date. The price of SR bought today is called the *spot rate,* or the rate at which they can be bought on the spot.

In Nov., 1996, the sport rate on SR was 0.841 IR per SR. On the same date one could contract to buy SRs within days in the future at the slightly higher price of 0.851 IR per SR—this later price is called forward price.

Now suppose that in late November '96, Cipla Ltd.'s financial manager is worried about the SR appreciating by December 31, 1996. Cipla Ltd. could enter into a contract to buy SR on December 31 at the forward price 0.851 IR Per SR. Again suppose that by December, 1996, the spot price has risen to 0.871. Cipla Ltd. can buy SR at the contractual price of 0.851, sell them at higher spot price of 0.871, and earn a profit of IR 16.1 million.

On December 31, the forward contract becomes due, buy 80824800 SRs at the agreed upon price of IR 8.851/SR

	IR	68781904
Less, Sell 824800 SR at the spot price of	0.871/SR	70398400
Profit in Indian Rupees	16.16496 Million IR	

This profit largely offsets the IR 24.2 million increase in Cipla's Sri Lankan debt as previously computed. This difference of Indian currency IR 808248 is Cipla's hedging cost.

A number of other methods of hedging against exchange losses on different types of liabilities and assets are available. Afterall, the important points for our purpose, are—(i) fluctuating exchange rates can cause earnings fluctuations for multinational corporations, but (ii) for a price, the financial manager can buy protection against this risk in the form of various types of hedges. In a world of floating exchange rates, managing assets and liabilities located all across the globe presents quite a challenge. The financial manager at corporate headquarters must not only anticipate currency realignments in each country, but also coordinate hedging strategies in all these countries.

CONCLUSION

The foregoing discussion highlighted various crucial factors in multinational finance. The financial management of the MNCs present more challenges than opportunities. Challenges in sense that their technical, financial and market network as well as risk bearing capacity are generally available in western developed world and multinationals of developing countries are facing their crucial financial management. They cannot complete with MNC so long as their foreign counterpart companies in managing the proper needed finance. In a world economy that grows more interdependent each year. The multinational manager can look forward to an ever expanding role in corporate decision making.

REFERENCES

1. Haner, F.T. Keiser, Stephen and Puglisi, Donald J-1981., *Introduction to Business Concept and Careers*, Winthrop Publisher INC Cambridge Massachusètt, p. 159-163.

2. Bonne, Louis E and David, L. Kurtz., *Contemporary Business*, The Dryden Press, Hinsdale, Illinois - 192-194.

3. Brigham, Eugene F., *Fundamentals of Financial Management*, The Dryden Press, Hinsdale, Illinois, p. 214.

4. Buffa, Elwood S. and Platcher, Barbara A.—Richard Dirwin INC, Homewood, Illinois, p-270-72.

5. Singh, L.P., *Global Caints*, Hindustan Times, Patna, 4th Sept.98, p-5.

6. Raghunathan, V., *Globalisation Economic* Era Economic Times, Calcutta, 31 Aug., 1998, p-4.

7. Singh, T.N., *Floating Capitalisation*, Business India, 9 Aug. '96, p-19.

8. Shrivastwa, R.M., *Financial Management and Policy*, Himalya Publishing, Mumbai, p-141-143.

9. Hull, J.C. and Hubbard, G.L., 1980—*Lease Evaluation in USA,* Journal of Business Finance and Accounting, p-48.

10. Pandey, R.M., *Multinationals in Financing,* Journal of Financial Management : April-June '97, p-19.

Forfaiting: Stutter Before the Run

Dr. Kanahalli Balappa*

Any businessman who is not already exporting will be hesitant to dip toe into what they practice as an ocean of boiling oil. The fear of distance, ocean barriers the difficulty of foreign barriers, the difficulty of foreign languages, customs and laws inhibit many from venturing into foreign markets. These presumed mysteries compel many exporters to trade only against letter of credit purchasing arrangements which restrict sales to only those importers who can or will tie up their funds to obtain letter of credit. This hampers the competitive strength of our exporters and country's exports are adversely affected. Though our government have evolved a system of providing guarantee and insurance facilities and also make available liberal export credit, yet the formalities involved in obtaining these facilities and the ultimate responsibility of exporter demotivate many businessmen from entering into foreign trade. Forfaiting relieves the exporters from the fear of credit losses and enables them to offer open accounts terms to overseas customers. It puts the exporter on an equal footing with the competition, both domestic and foreign.[1]

Keeping the above in view, a brief attempt is made to show, why forfaiting stutter before it run.

FORFAITING

Forfaiting enables exporters to convert their credit sales into cash sales by discounting their receivables with an agency—a forfaiter. The exporter is thus able to receive cash immediately despite offering the buyer extended credit terms. On the other hand, forfaiting alleviates country commercial,

* Senior Lecturer and Faculty Member, Department of Commerce, Gulbarga University, Gulbarga.

transfer and documentary. Exchange and interest risk inherent in international transactions, simplifies documentation and hence, speeds up trade finance decision. Right now, five outfits in India offer forfaiting services. These are Hongkong Bank, Indo Aval, ABN AMRO Bank, Meghraj Financials and Net West Bank. These outfits have alliances with international forfaiting agencies.[2]

BENEFITS OF FORFAITING

Forfaiting offers the following benefits

No approval is required for longer credit period

Credit period for the Indian exporters is limited to 180 days of shipment. For deferred credit period beyond 180 days,.the exporter has to obtain RBI's permission that involves several procedural hassles, due to this there is a chance of losing clients who expects longer credit terms. This type of problem is not there under forfaiting. Under this, exporters can avail credit periods of 4-7 years without knocking the door of RBI as they can receive the export proceeds within the stipulated time.

It overcomes the risk of fraud

A trade transaction involves a great deal of documentation, the process of authentication at each stage assumes a great importance. The forfaiting agency will ensure that the various documents are valid in order to protect its investment. Therefore, the exporter can totally ignore the risk of fraud.

Forfaiting cost is viable

The cost paid by the exporter to forfaiter is competitive enough with the post shipment credit rates in case he is exporting to places where country risk is low. For instance, the cost of forfaiting a 6month export receivable to the UK may workout to 13.5 per cent, while the port shipment credit rates are in the range of 13-15 per cent. In case of African countries, the forfaiting cost could be anywhere between 15-25 per cent. However, considering the risk involved in receiving the receivables and the premium charged by our exporters, the forfaiting cost is viable.

Boon for the exports

For exporting to a particular country, the exporter bank requires Export Credit Guarantee Cooperation (ECGC) cover to export his goods. Such type of cover is not required under forfaiting. Therefore, forfaiting acts as a boon for the exporters selling their products to a country for which ECGC doesn't offer cover.

IMPEDIMENTS TO FORFAITING IN INDIA

Despite the numerous benefits that would flow from forfaiting, progress on this count is rather very slow in India. It is, therefore, essential to identify the reason for this. The important ones are as follows:

Lack of awareness

The main reason for forfaiting not catching up in India is lack of awareness among the exporting community. Neither governments nor banks have taken steps to popularize this exporting tool. Exporters in India simply don't know that they can avail of a product, which offer them liquidity through export financing as well as eliminates the inherent risks involved in international trade.

High cost of forfaiting

The cost of forfaiting has elements of cost such as cost of finance and cost of risk. This amount is payable to the forfaiter, the movement the export receivables are forfaited. These costs in turn would add up to the cost of exports. Due to this, exports will not be competitive and in addition, exporters will lose their expected margin. Therefore, exporters in India are price conscious and do not want to lose their margin. This in fact as a stumbling block for the development of forfaiting business in India.

Indian banks prefer post-shipment credit to forfaiting

Another important reason for the problem of forfaiting in India is that, banks are reluctant to promote forfaiting as it obviates the need for post-shipment credit. According to RBI guidelines, banks are expected to achieve an export credit target of 12 per cent. Despite the fact that forfaiting falls outside the purview of bank finance and exporters can avail of both post-shipment credit and forfaiting. Indian exporters usually use forfaiting as an alternative for post-shipment credit. When this is the case, banks naturally would prefer post-shipment credit to forfaiting because through this banker can earn better income and meet export targets.[3]

Depreciation of rupee

Depreciation of rupee is another threat, why forfaiting is not catching up in India. Bankers contend that exporters are willing to forfait their receivables from short-term to medium term, where as globally, the average period is from 5 to 7 years. Exporters, who are willing to go for longer-term exports, bank on depreciation of rupee. This assumption appears to be right since the Indian rupee on an average depreciates by 5 per cent in a year. As a result, forfaiting in India is generally used for a six months to two-year tenor, where as exporters with longer credit period's stick to post-shipment credit.[4]

Lack of adequate database

The pre-requisite for the conduct of forfaiting business is that the forfaiter require information with regard to importing countries, importers, their respective country's currency etc. With reference to this, Indian forfaiting agencies have an inadequate information base. Therefore, it has becoming a stumbling block for the progress of forfaiting in India.

Absence of flawless legal framework

Apart from the above-mentioned problems, there is another problem for forfaiting in India is that, the absence of flawless legal framework. Contrary to this, the forfaiting in US is in maturity, as there is a well-established legal framework to conduct the business.

In fine, we can say that forfaiting, as an alternate source of trade finance especially for deferred exports is likely to become popular over a period of time. The present thrust of country is to more towards an era of export promotion in the process of which, forfaiting has a very important role to play. With the likely introduction of forfaiting service by the EXIM bank, the movement would obviously receive the required impetus. Therefore an attempt must be made to overcome the practical problems mentioned above. If these were to be allowed to remain, forfaiting definitely stutter before it runs successfully.

REFERENCES

1. Narender Kumar, *Export Factoring: Its Prospects in India*, Management of Financial Services, 1996.

2. Narayana Murthy, A.Y., *Forfaiting out of Slumber, Chartered Financial Analyst*, June 1997.

3. *Ibid.*

4. *Ibid.*

Industrial Finance By State Financial Corporations —An Analytical Study of Andhra Pradesh State Financial Corporation

Dr. D. Himachalam *
C. Viswanadha Reddy **

The economic prosperity of the country depends upon the development of agriculture as well as industrial sectors. The development of agricultural sector requires adequate irrigation facilities, manpower, farm credit and so on but the industrial sector requires not only machinery and equipment but also skilled manpower, energy, banking, marketing and transportation facilities. All these infrastructure facilities and services are vital for economic development. Among all these, finance plays a crucial role as it is the pre-requisite and forms the basis for all the key inputs. Without finance nothing will progress and the industrial activity will grind to halt. Generally finance is required at various stages of industrial activity viz.,

i. to meet initial start-up needs,
ii. to meet working capital needs, and
iii. to meet research and developmental needs.

To meet the ever-increasing financial needs of the industrial sector and to accelerate its development, a large number of specialised financial institutions also called Development Financial Institutions (DFI's) have been setup in the country after independence. The role of these DFI's is to mobilise scarce resources viz., capital, technology, and entrepreneurial and managerial talents and to channelise these resources into productive

* Associate Professor, Department of Commerce, S.V. University Post-graduate Centre, Kavali - 524 201 (A.P.)

** Research Scholar, Department of Commerce, S.V. University Post-graduate Centre, Kavali - 524 201 (A.P.)

purposes. In fact, economic prosperity and industrial development will also depend on efficient management of funds by banks. Efficient management of these institutions will not only improve their profitability but also enhance their contribution to industrial development. All India Development Banks like IDBI, ICICI, IFCI, IRBI, SCICI provide financial assistance to medium and large-scale industries. Small Industries Development Bank of India caters to the needs of small and tiny units at the central level. At the state level SFCs provide financial assistance mainly to small and medium enterprises, whereas Small Industry Development Corporations cater to the needs of medium and large industries at their respective states.

FOCUS OF THE PROBLEM

In view of the limited scope of the operations of Industrial Finance Corporation of India to cater the long-term credit needs of small and medium scale industrial units, private and public limited companies in corporate sector, the SFCs assume greater importance in extending long term financial assistance to small and medium scale units. Thus SFCs buckled down to purvey both financial and managerial assistance to the industrial units in their respective states. Hence, a study on the progress and performance of SFCs in different dimensions in extending financial assistance assumes significance in this context. Keeping this in view, an attempt is made to study the financial performance of SFCs in relation to DFIs, the place of APSFC in relation to SFCs in general and the operational performance of APSFC in particular.

OBJECTIVES OF THE STUDY

The specific objectives of the study are as follows:

1. To examine the contribution of Development Banks in industrial financing.
2. To study the trend in sanctions and disbursements made by APSFC
3. To assess the various issues in industrial financing by APSFC

METHODOLOGY

The APSFC has been purposefully selected for the present study in view of its successful functioning over the period of 4 decades. The corporation is a premier term lending institutions in the State. In order to serve the existing and prospective entrepreneurs who are spread all over the state, the Corporation functions through its 25 branch offices, 2 field offices and 4 zonal offices apart from its Head Office at Hyderabad. The study is based on the secondary data for the period from 1986-87 to 1995-96; collected from the various issues of annual reports and personal contacts with the officials of APSFC, economic survey, Government of India. In the analysis and interpretation of data, statistical techniques like percentages, averages, growth rates, quotients, Pearson's co-efficient of correlation, standard deviation, chained index numbers, regression analysis, t-test, have been used.

RESULTS AND DISCUSSION

Position of State Financial Corporations

The SFCs have successfully completed more than 40 years in the fulfillment of its avowed objectives. In the process of serving the nation they have emerged as a major source of industrial finance at regional level. It occupies an importance place in the industrial scene as it provides major chunk of funds to the industry. The place of SFCs in the structure of DFIs in India is furnished in Table—1. (See Table—1 in Page no. 113).

It is clear from the table that the SFCs have accounted 9 and 10 per cent of aggregate sanctions and disbursements respectively made by DFIs as on 31st March, 1994. During the period of 10 years, the sanctions of SFCs have increased from Rs. 1009.1 crores to 2760.2 crores and the disbursements has increased from 608.5 crores to 2005.4 crores. However, it is piquant to note that the growth in SFCs assistance to industrial sector is not commensurate with the growth of DFIs assistance. For instance, the DFIs assistance increased from Rs. 2543.7 crores in 1980-81 to 60,522 crores in 1994-95 accounting for 23 fold increase during the 14 year period, where as the growth in sanctions made by SFCs recorded at 9 fold only.

APPLICATION OF t-TEST

The null and alternative hypothesis kept in view and also the results of the t-test are briefly discussed hereunder.

TABLE—1

Assistance Sanctioned and Disbursed by DFIs Vis-A-Vis SFCs (Rs. in Crores)

Year	Sanctions By DFIs	Link Relative	Sanctions By SFC's	Link Relative	Disbursements By DFI's	Link Relative	Disbursements By SFC's	Link Relative	6 As percentage of 2	8 As percentage of
1	2	3	4	5	6	7	8	9	10	11
1980-81	2543.7		370.5		1858.4		248.0			
1985-86	7511.8	100	1009.1	100	5608.4	100	608.5	100	74.66	60.25
1986-87	9072.6	120	1210.8	119	6604.1	117	791.9	130	72.80	65.37
1987-88	10288.3	113	1305.0	107	7687.9	116	972.5	122	74.72	74.48
1988-89	15299.9	148	1391.9	106	10084.5	131	1085.0	112	66.00	78.00
1989-90	16639.0	108	1514.2	108	11058.9	109	1186.5	106	66.46	76.35
1990-91	21590.2	129	1863.9	123	14701.6	133	1270.8	110	68.10	68.17
1991-92	26135.1	121	2190.3	117	18729.8	127	1536.8	121	71.66	70.14
1992-93	36478.5	139	2025.4	92	25711.6	137	1569.7	102	70.48	77.48
1993-94	42155.8	115	1908.8	94	27647.8	107	1563.4	100	65.60	81.92
1994-95	60522.0	143	2760.2	144	33625.3	121	2005.4	128	55.56	72.64
			$\overline{X}$ = 1717.96 σ = 159.35 CV = 9.27				$\overline{Y}$ =1250.05 σ =127.14 CV =10.17		$\overline{X}_1$ = 68.63	$\overline{X}_2$ = 72.48
Correlation Co-efficient=0.98										

Source : Economic Survey: 1995-96.

The null hypothesis (Ho): There is no significant difference between the disbursement ratio of SFCs and other DFIs as a whole during the study period.

The alternative hypothesis (Ha) : There is a significant difference between the disbursement ratio of SFCs and other SFCs during the study period.

Result : The t-value is calculated by using the following formula:

$$t = \frac{\overline{X}_1 - \overline{X}_2}{S} \sqrt{\frac{n_1 n_2}{n_1 + n_2}}$$

t= 1.288

Since, the calculated 't' value is 1.288 which is less than the table value of 't' at 18 degrees of freedom and at 5 per cent level of significance ($v=18, t_{0.05}=2.101$) the null hypothesis of no difference between the disbursements ratio of SFCs and other DFIs is holds good. Therefore, it is concluded that the difference between the disbursement ratio of SFCs and other DFIs in the country is not statistically significant and the SFCs are not different from other DFIs in respect of disbursements ratio during the study period.

From the observations made above, it is clear that though the growth in assistance made by SFCs is not on par in the DFIs, the SFCs are recorded a continuous positive growth in the sanctions and disbursements through out the study period.

TRENDS IN SANCTIONS AND DISBURSEMENTS BY APSFC

The APSFC occupied a prominent place among the all SFCs in the country because of its praiseworthy performance in the areas of sanctions and disbursements. The detailed information regarding the sanctions and disbursements made by APSFC is furnished in Table—2.

The purpose of this analysis is to examine the trend in sanctions, disbursements and disbursements ratio achieved by the corporation in its efforts to promote industrial growth during the study period. The table reveals that, during the period under study, the growth in respect of

TABLE—2

Trends in Amount of Sanctions and Disbursements made by APSFC (Rs. in Crores)

Year	Sanctions	Annual Growth	Disbursements	Annual Growth	Disbursements Ratio	Disbursements Ratio of Other SFCs
1986-87	135.34	—	81.02	—	59.60	65.37
1987-88	131.83	-2.56	102.49	26.50	77.71	74.48
1988-89	169.57	28.58	113.24	10.49	66.78	78.00
1989-90	194.88	14.23	127.87	12.89	65.60	76.35
1990-91	265.30	36.13	144.74	13.22	55.56	68.17
1991-92	218.13	-17.78	157.25	8.64	72.09	70.14
1992-93	194.65	-10.76	132.53	-15.72	68.09	77.48
1993-94	91.40	-52.77	82.07	-38.07	89.72	81.92
1994-95	138.83	51.89	87.73	6.90	63.19	72.04
1995-96	186.90	34.62	116.81	33.14	62.50	64.41
	$\overline{X} = 172.69$ $\sigma = 15.05$ CV = 8.72		$\overline{Y} = 114.57$ $\sigma = 7.93$ CV =6.92		$\overline{X}_1 = 68.08$	$\overline{X}_2 = 72.90$
	Correlation Co-efficient =0.9					

Source : Various issues of Annual Reports of APSFC.

sanctions and disbursements is not satisfactory. This situation may be because of poor resource mobilisation and recovery of loans by APSFC. The growth rate in sanctions varies between 52.77 per cent and 51.89 per cent and the growth rate in respect of disbursements vary between 38.07 per cent and 33.14 per cent. The disbursement ratio of APSFC ranges between 55.36 per cent and 89.72 per cent. The Correlation Co-efficient between sanctions and disbursements is 0.9 indicating a positive correlation between sanctions and disbursements.

APPLICATION OF t-TEST

The null hypothesis (Ho) : There is no significant variation between the disbursements ratio of APSFC and other SFC's as a whole during the study period.

The alternative hypothesis (Ha) : There is a significant variation between the disbursement ratio of APSFC and other SFCs during the study period.

Result: The value calculated is 1.333 which is lesser than the table value at 18 degrees of freedom and at 5 per cent level of significance ($v=18$; $t_{0.05}=2.101$), the null hypothesis of 'no difference' holds good. In other words, the difference between the disbursement ratio of APSFC and other SFCs in the country is not statistically significant.

THE LOAN AMOUNT APPLIED AND LOAN AMOUNT SANCTIONED

This type of analysis indicates the performance of the APSFC in extending its financial services to meet the demand for loan from existing as well as prospective entrepreneurs. The amount of loan applied indicates the demand for loan assistance from the side of entrepreneurs whereas the amount of loan sanctioned indicates the extent of demand satisfied by the Corporation.

From the Table—3 it can be noticed that, the average sanctions in relation to amount applied had recorded 69.90 per cent during the period under review. The Standard Deviation of loan amount applied (σX) is 2417.92 and the Co-efficient of Variation (CV of X) is 9.29. The Standard Deviation of loan amount sanctioned (σY) is 1617.80 and the Co-efficient of Variation (CV of Y) is 8.92. Thus, it indicates that the deviation in loan amount applied is higher than in loan amount sanctioned. The Pearson's

TABLE—3

Loan Amount Applied and Loan Amount Sanctioned by APSFC (Rs in lakhs)

Year	Loan Amount Applied		Loan Amount Sanctioned		4 As Percentage of 2	5 As Percentage oF 3
	No. of Applications	Amount	No. of Applications	Amount		
1986-87	3178	18541.59	2597	13661.29	81.72	73.63
1987-88	4561	21134.77	3657	13184.41	80.18	62.38
1988-89	4486	22994.81	3658	17756.80	81.54	77.22
1989-90	7011	27795.22	6002	20051.17	85.61	72.14
1990-91	13566	40374.39	12065	27694.60	88.94	68.54
1991-92	7449	35983.71	5914	22908.58	71.39	63.66
1992-93	4713	30316.39	3620	21465.97	76.80	70.81
1993-94	1933	15009.47	1384	9685.99	71.60	64.33
1994-95	1552	19627.99	1297	14739.68	83.56	75.10
1995-96	1732	28602.14	1391	20302.51	80.31	70.98
		$\overline{X}$ = 26038.05 σ = 2417.92 CV = 9.29		$\overline{Y}$ = 18142.10 σ = 1617.80 CV = 8.92	$\overline{X}_1$ = 80.97	$\overline{X}_2$ = 69.90

Correlation Co-efficient 0.976

Regression equation of Y on X = 0.65x + 1217.37

Regression equation of X on Y= 1.46y– 449.42

Source: Various issues of Annual Reports of APSFC.

Co-efficient of correlation in between the loan amount applied and the loan amount sanctioned is 0.976, which indicates a positive correlation.

APPLICATION OF t-TEST

The null hypothesis (Ho): The loan amount sanctioned by APSFC is closely associated with the loan amount applied by the entrepreneurs.

The alternative hypothesis (Ha): The loan amount sanctioned by APSFC is not closely associated with the loan amount applied by the entrepreneurs.

Result: The t-value for Correlation Co-efficient can be calculated based on the formula

$$t = \frac{r}{\sqrt{1-r^2}} \times \sqrt{n-2}$$ where r= Correlation Co-efficient.

is 18.89 which is much higher than the table value at 18 degrees of freedom and at 5 per cent level of significance ($v=18$, $t_{0.05} = 2.101$), so the alternative hypothesis of 'not closely associated' holds true.

TRENDS IN FORMS OF FINANCIAL ASSISTANCE

The analysis of trends in forms of financial assistance rendered by the Corporation is necessary to ascertain to what extent the Corporation has rendered the assistance to the entrepreneurs. The analysis helps to bring out its functioning like a DFI or just as a term lending institution.

The Table—4 furnishes the data pertaining to the various forms of financial assistance rendered by the Corporation during the period and the cumulative up to 31 March, 1996. It can be observed from the table that the Corporation has rendered a maximum assistance in the form of term loans in each year followed by the working capital assistance. The term loans were given highest priority with the maximum amount of Rs. 148815.54 lakhs accounting for 96.03 per cent followed by the working capital assitance of Rs. 1803.17 lakhs accounting for 1.17 per cent. Special capital assistance occupied next place with an amount of Rs. 1643.9 lakhs (1.08 per cent), bridge finance with an amount of Rs. 966.27 lakhs (0.63 per cent) in relation to the cumulative assistance Rs. 153523.28 lakhs rendered by the Corporation up to the end of 31 March, 1996.

TABLE—4

Classification of Different Forms of Financial Assistance Rendered by APSFC (Rs in Lakhs)

Sl. No	Form of Loans	1987-88	1989-90	1991-92	1993-94	1995-96	Cumulative since inception to March 31st, 1996
1	Term Loans	9908.83 (96.7)	12429.58 (97.2)	14896.83 (94.7)	7994.63 (97.4)	11608.34 (99.38)	148815.84 (96.93)
2.	Working Capital Loans	—	35.23 (0.30)	621.94 (4.00)	191.22 (2.30)	76.42 (0.62)	1803.17 (1.17)
3	Bridge Loans	116.39 (1.10)	125.94 (1.00)	—	—	—	966.27 (0.63)
4	Under writing of shares	—	—	—	—	—	65.12 (0.04)
5.	Under writing of debentures	—	—	—	—	—	34.00 (0.02)
6	Subscription to shares and debentures	—	—	—	—	—	195.39 (0.13)
7	Special Capital Assistance	223.71 (2.20)	193.40 (1.50)	206.55 (1.30)	20.85 (0.30)	—	1643.90 (1.08)
	Total	10248.93	12784.15	15725.32	8206.70	11680.76	153523.38

Note: Figures in brackets indicates percentages to total.
Source: Various issues of Annual Reports of APSFC.

CONSTITUTION—WISE ANALYSIS OF LOANS SANCTIONED AND DISBURSED

The SFCs were started when the IFCI ceases its operations to cater the long term financial needs of SSIs, private and public limited companies in corporate sector, co-operatives, partnership and sole proprietary concerns etc. The constitution-wise analysis of term loans assisted would help to find out whether the APSFC playing the gap-filling role satisfactorily or not.

Table 5 furnishes the da ta concerning to the constitution wise term loans sanctioned and disbursed by APSFC. The major share had gone to the private limited companies ranged between 33.77 per cent and 52.66 per cent, to public limited companies are ranged between 2.53 per cent and 8.94 per cent, to cooperatives 0.1 per cent and 0.3 per cent, to partnership concerns 15.15 per cent and 23.08 per cent and sole proprietary concerns 23.79 per cent and 43.79 per cent. The table also furnishes the information about the average annual percentage of assistance to the various constitutional clients. It indicates that, high margin of assistance had gone to the private limited companies (45.17 per cent) followed by sole proprietary concerns (30.55 per cent) and partnership concerns (19.08 per cent).

On the other hand, the share of assistance disbursed by the Corporation to public limited companies ranged between 3.01 per cent and 8.94 per cent, to private limited companies ranged between 35.16 per cent and 51.62 per cent, to partnership concerns ranged between 15.53 per cent and 22.88 per cent and to sole proprietary concerns ranged between 22.61 per cent and 39.98 per cent. On an average, out of total disbursements, the high proportion i.e 45.12 per cent was availed by the private limited companies followed by sole concerns with 30.64 per cent and partnership concerns with 19.01 per cent. Therefore, it can be clearly observed from the above analysis, that the major beneficiaries of the assistance from the Corporation are private limited companies followed by sole concerns and partnership concerns.

APSFC ASSISTANCE TO SMALL - SCALE SECTOR

SFCs Act laid emphasis on SFCs to cater the financial needs of small and medium scale enterprises. Therefore, the promotion of SSIs is directly

TABLE—5

Constitution-wise Classification of Term Loans Sanctioned (Effective) and Disbursed

(Rs. 8 Lakshs)

Sl No	Constitution	1988-89		1989-90		1991-92		1993-94		1995-96		Mean Percentage	
1	2	3	4	5	6	7	8	9	10	11	12	13	14
1	Public Ltd. Companies	918.15 (5.61)	944.94 (8.94)	852.82 (4.61)	769.60 (6.19)	714.09 (3.47)	598.63 (4.02)	361.36 (3.84)	255.46 (3.19)	1384.83 (7.69)	931.27 (8.02)	(4.89)	(5.00)
2	Private Ltd. Companies	8623.99 (52.66)	537.80 (50.89)	8484.85 (45.86)	5618.55 (45.20)	8573.45 (41.70)	5237.65 (35.16)	4370.21 (47.46)	3670.34 (45.91)	8352.31 (46.40)	5261.46 (45.32)	(45.17)	(45.12)
3	Co-operatives	—	6.17 (0.06)	—	2.75 (0.02)	100.67 (0.49)	2.58 (0.02)	38.07 (0.40)	11.88 (0.15)	8.99 (0.05)	7.74 (0.07)	(0.26)	(0.07)
4	Partnership Concerns	—	2481.82 (15.15)	1842.36 (17.44)	3053.31 (16.50)	2346.86 (16.79)	4463.45 (21.71)	2887.39 (22.89)	1872.05 (19.90)	3894.32 (21.63)	2554.17 (22.00)	(19.08)	(19.03)
5	Sole Proprietary Concerns	4327.34 (26.42)	2839.09 (22.61)	6112.02 (33.03)	4025.94 (32.39)	6708.12 (32.63)	5956.18 (39.98)	27650.5 (29.44)	2422.54 (30.32)	4282.55 (23.79)	2769.71 (23.86)	(30.55)	(30.64)
6	Others	27.04 (0.16)	6.55 (0.06)	— —	4.50 (0.01)	0.27 (0.00)	0.06 (0.00)	—	—	78.15 (0.44)	8.99 (0.73)	(0.05)	(0.13)
	Total	16377.64	10565.91	18503.00	125429.58	20560.05	14896.83	9407.20	7994.63	18001.15	11608.34		

Note : Figures in brackets indicates percentages to total

Source : Annual Reports of APSFC.

resulted in equitable distribution of national income, wealth, economic opportunities and economic power. Towards this end the APSFC too has to play an important role in the industrialisation of Andhra Pradesh particularly in promoting SSIs.

TABLE—6
APSFC Assistance to Small-Scale Sector

(Rs. in lakhs)

Year	Total Sanctions		Sanctions to SSI Units		Percentage in Relation to Total	
	No. of Units	Amount	No. of Units	Amount	No. of Units	Amount
1986-87	2597	13251.51	2416	8485.48	95	64.03
1987-88	3657	12732.16	3518	8210.25	96	64.48
1988-89	3658	16555.26	3392	11937.41	92	72.10
1989-90	5510	18503.00	5324	14701.69	96	79.46
1990-91	9388	24658.34	9197	19272.88	98	78.16
1991-92	4699	20560.05	4467	16001.89	95	77.88
1992-93	3389	18899.67	3144	15475.21	93	81.88
1993-94	1449	9407.20	1333	7869.67	92	83.65
1994-95	1206	13970.91	1077	11070.40	89	79.24
1995-96	1317	18001.15	1187	14397.42	90	80.00
	51552	161470.44	49357	122196.06	96	76.00

Source: Compiled from the Annual Reports APSFC.

Table—6 depicts Aspics assistance to small-scale sector. It reveals that, a considerable large amount of assistance is sanctioned by APSFC to small-scale sector. The number of small-scale units assisted by the Corporation in relation to the total number of units assisted, ranged between 89 per cent and 98 per cent. The amount sanctioned by APSFC to small-scale sector also ranged between 64.03 per cent and 83.65 per cent in relation to total sanctions. As on 31 march, 1996 the total number of units assisted by the Corporation are 51,552, out of which the number of small-scale units were 49,357 accounting for 96 per cent of the total number of units.

The total amount of assistance sanctioned by the Corporation, as on 31 March 1996 was Rs. 161470.44 lakhs, out of which the small-scale units are claimed Rs. 122196.06 lakhs accounting for 76 per cent to the total sanctions.

AREA-WISE CLASSIFICATION OF TERM LOANS SANCTIONED AND DISBURSED BY APSFC

It is essential to examine the importance accorded by APSFC to develop the notified backward areas in Andhra Pradesh. Table—7 exhibits the area-wise classification of assistance made by the corporation during the study period. Area-wise classification consists of Backward areas declared by the Central Government (as per location) into Category A,B and C. Backward areas declared by the State Government (as per location) and the other areas which are not covered under first two Categories. The APSFC sanctions to Centrally backward areas under Category—B ranged between 22.06 per cent and 49.80 per cent and the disbursements ranged between 20.45 per cent and 45.44 per cent out of the total assistance. The sanctions to Category–C ranged between 4.46 per cent and 19.38 per cent and the disbursements ranged between 8.06 per cent and 16.93 per cent respectively. On an average, the APSFC sanctions to centrally backward areas are 40.36 per cent and disbursements 43.49 per cent out of total assistance during the study period.

The Corporations sanctions to backward areas declared by the State Government ranged between 6.04 per cent and 32.79 per cent and disbursements between 6.87 per cent 30.12 per cent. Out of the total assistance, 17.44 per cent in case of sanctions and 19.36 per cent in case of disbursements are recorded on an average. On the other hand, on an average the areas, which are not covered under the first and second categories, claimed 39.07 per cent in case of sanctions and 40.28 per cent in case of disbursements. From the above analysis, we can observe that the APSFC made nearly 60 per cent of its total assistance to backward areas to achieve balanced regional development.

INDUSTRY-WISE ANALYSIS OF TERM LOANS SANCTIONED BY APSFC

The SFCs in India provides assistance to various categories of Industrial units from small artistic nature of entrepreneurs to the sophisticated lines of manufacturers. Proper industrial plan in any State should envisage diversification in its industrial base. Keeping in view the need for diversified industrial activity, an attempt is made to analyse the performance of APSFC in providing assistance to various categories of industries in Andhra Pradesh. For the purpose of analysis, various

TABLE—7

Area-wise Classification of Term Loans Sanctioned and Disbursed (Rs. Lakhs)

Sl. No.	Particulars	1988-89		1991-92		1993-94		1995-96		Average	
1	Backward areas declared by Central Govt.										
	Category—A	–	–	–	–	–	–	–	–	–	–
	Category—B	8156.51 (49.80)	5005.09 (45.44)	4541.91 (22.10)	4147.17 (27.14)	2115.69 (27.35)	2186.19 (27.35)	5478.26 (30.43)	3697.74 (31.85)	(27.86)	(30.32)
	Category—C	2238.63 (13.67)	1741.02 (15.80)	2298.39 (11.18)	2080.23 (14.66)	1529.74 (16.26)	1074.28 (13.44)	3489.67 (19.38)	1964.98 (16.93)	(12.50)	(13.17)
2	Backward Areas Declared by the State Govt.	988.83 (6.04)	756.47 (6.87)	4578.43 (22.27)	2921.57 (19.61)	3084.61 (32.79)	2407.88 (30.12)	2002.58 (11.12)	1846.85 (15.91)	(19.36)	(17.44)
3.	Other Areas not covered under 1 & 2	4993.67 (30.49)	3513.33 (31.89)	9141.32 (44.95)	5747.86 (38.59)	2677.16 (28.46)	2326.28 (29.09)	7030.64 (39.07)	4098.77 (35.31)	(40.28)	(39.07)
	Total	16377.64	11015.91	20360.05	14896.83	9407.20	7994.63	18001.15	11608.34		

Note : Figures in brackets indicates percentages to total

Source: Annual Reports of APSFC

industries financed by the Corporation have been broadly classified into three categories. They are traditional agro-based industries, Basic and capital goods industries and service and other industries.

TABLE—8

Industry-wise Classification of Loans Sanctioned (Both Small-scale and Other Units)

(Rs Lakhs)

Year	Traditional Industries	Basic and Capital Goods Industries	Service and Other Industries	Total
1986-87	2708.89 (20.44)	8690.16 (65.58)	1852.46 (13.98)	13251.51
1987-88	3443.41 (27.04)	6719.66 (52.78)	2569.09 (20.18)	12732.16
1988-89	3753.66 (22.93)	7852.06 (47.94)	4771.92 (29.14)	16377.64
1989-90	4367.99 (23.60)	8459.32 (45.72)	5675.69 (30.67)	18503.00
1990-91	5144.18 (28.91)	11388.32 (45.49)	6189.08 (25.10)	24658.34
1991-92	6694.20 (32.55)	9238.09 (44.95)	4627.76 (22.50)	20560.05
1992-93	5696.17 (30.14)	8767.49 (46.39)	4436.01 (23.47)	18899.67
1993-94	3059.40 (32.52)	3796.12 (40.35)	2551.68 (27.13)	9407.20
1994-95	4114.80 (29.45)	6651.36 (47.60)	3204.75 (22.95)	13970.91
1995-96	55.3.94 (29.25)	8303.23 (46.15)	4388.98 (24.10)	18001.95
Cumulative as on 31st March, 1996	46488.83 (28.79)	74827.47 (46.34)	40154.14 (24.87)	161470.44

Note: Figures in brackets indicates percentages to total
Source: Annual Reports of APSFC.

The following points can be noted from the data furnished in the Table—8.

1. The traditional and agro-based industries occupied a prominent place in the total sanctions made by the Corporation. Its assistance to this category increased from Rs. 2708.89 lakhs in 1986-87 to 5304.94 lakhs in 1995-96 and the same had ranged between 20.44 per cent and 32.55 per cent to the total. In this category, the industries like Food products had gained major share of assistance followed by textile industries and paper product industries.
2. The another category of Basic and Capital Goods industries had been claimed a major share of assistance throughout the period under study. The amount of sanctions flown to this category ranged between 40.35 per cent and 65.58 per cent during the period under review. In this category, the industries like chemical products, non-metallic and

mineral products are continued to claim a bulk of assistance by the Corporation.

3. The assistance sanctioned by the Corporation to the categories of services and other industries do not exhibit a clear trend during the study period.

From the observations, it can be noted that, out of the total assistance made by the Corporation, only few industries like food products, textiles, chemicals have continued to draw bulk of assistance, but the remaining categories of industries have not received adequate share of assistance.

ZONE-WISE ANALYSIS OF TERM LOANS SANCTIONED

Analysis of Zone-wise operations of APSFC helps to observe the inter-zone variations in assistance rendered by APSFC.

Data relating to Zone-wise analysis of loans sanctioned during the period of 10 years ending at 31st March 1996 is furnished in Table No—9. By making through analysis of data the following observations are made.

For administrative convenience the state Andhra Pradesh have divided into five Zones viz., Hyderabad, Warangal, Visakhapatnam, Vijayawada and Tirupati. Among all five zones, out of total assistance sanctioned by the Corporation as on 31st March, 1996 of Rs. 161470.44 lakhs. Hyderabad zone had received major share of 38.93 per cent followed by Tirupati zone (18.78 per cent), Vijayawada zone (14.64 per cent), Visakhapatnam zone (14.12 per cent) and Warangal zone (13.53 per cent). It is evident that there is a wide variation in assistance rendered by the Corporation among all districts of various zones. The Corporation had paid more attention on the districts located nearby the state capital only, which leads to imbalanced regional development.

PROBLEMS OF STATE FINANCIAL CORPORATIONS

Commendable though, the above contribution towards the industrial development of Andhra Pradesh, it is not meeting the financial needs of the entrepreneurs fully due to the various problems. And it not raising up to expectations to match the financial demands with its financial services in the way to achieve to its avowed objectives towards rapid industrialisation. It is severely facing the problems of dearth of financial resources, improper project execution, red tapism in sanctioning the projects, imbalanced dispersal of industries, too much dependence on IDBI, poor monitoring of the project, poor recovery performance and the like. While it is necessary to formulate proper plans and establish effective control over their operations, it is equally important to remove the difficulties facing them.

TABLE—9

Zone-wise Classification of Loans Sanctioned (Rs. in lakhs)

Year	Zone-I Hyderabad	Zone-II Warangal	Zone-III Visakha-patnam	Zone-IV Vijaya-wada	Zone-V Tirupati	Grand Total
1986-87	3179.40	1545.73	1471.93	1326.10	2983.35	10506.51
	(30.26)	(14.71)	(14.00)	(12.62)	(28.41)	
1987-88	4632.64	1581.37	1870.66	1944.90	2742.59	12732.16
	(36.39)	(12.42)	(14.38)	(15.26)	(21.55)	
1988-89	7380.18	1807.85	1758.79	1974.24	3456.58	16377.64
	(45.06)	(11.04)	(10.74)	(12.05)	(21.11)	
1989-90	7080.98	2914.98	2252.63	2622.93	3631.48	18503.00
	(38.27)	(15.75)	(12.17)	(14.18)	(19.63)	
1990-91	8446.19	3964.34	2856.27	4180.75	5210.79	24658.34
	(39.25)	(16.08)	(11.58)	(16.95)	(21.14)	
1991-92	6913.84	3706.94	2330.42	3481.96	4126.89	20560.05
	(33.63)	(18.03)	(11.33)	(16.94)	(20.07)	
1992-93	8046.45	3289.41	1719.32	2577.07	3267.42	18899.67
	(42.57)	(17.40)	(9.10)	(13.64)	(17.29)	
1993-94	3675.82	1060.73	1165.88	1802.83	1701.94	9407.20
	(39.07)	(11.28)	(12.39)	(19.16)	(18.10)	
1994-95	6452.32	1176.08	1975.68	1942.33	2424.50	13970.91
	(46.18)	(8.42)	(14.14)	(13.90)	(17.36)	
1995-96	7455.35	1809.12	3158.73	222.39	3355.56	18001.15
	(41.42)	(10.05)	(17.55)	(12.35)	(18.63)	
Total as on 31st Mar. '96	62865.64 (38.93)	21842.89 (13.53)	22794.65 (14.12)	23642.34 (14.64)	30324.92 (18.78)	161470.44

Note : Figures in brackets indicates percentages to total

Source: Annual Reports of APSFC.

RESOURCE CONSTRAINTS

The main hindrance in the steady progress of SFCs is inadequacy of financial resources. It is necessary to raise more funds by searching for new sources. At present the APSFC is mainly depending on debt capital. The proportion of debt in total resource structure ranged between a maximum of 90.9 per cent and a minimum of 83.4 per cent and equity constitutes nearly 9 to 10 per cent during the period under review. In this context the corporation has to give weightage to the leverage impact on its profitability. If the leverage gives positive impact, the Corporation can go for any amount of debt or vice-versa. Therefore, a good and complete exercise in resource planning for short term as well as long term periods is of utmost need of the Corporation in order to cater to the growing financial needs of industrial concerns.

RECOVERY OF ARREARS

SFCs have to recover their past loans. The real test of their performance lies in recovery of loans rather than in granting of loans. Recovery is of utmost importance for SFCs as in the long run, it is the main source, which can make further loaning possible. The loans granted by SFCs are said to be made in the right direction only when they are able to get repayment of such loans. The bulk of SFCs funds are blocked in over dues. Quantitatively, SFCs the progress of loan is not much alarming but qualitatively it is very poor and their operations do not serve the desired object. It is, course, true that some industrial units do not repay because of genuine difficulties but huge arrears which SFCs have shown proves that most loanees think that SFCs loans need not be repaid. This state of affairs indicates not only faulty sanctions to projects without taking adequate care about recovery but also inefficient management.

In order to improve the repayment position of industrial concerns, it is essential to introduce some strict measures against defaulters. The recovery staff should be made personally accountable for the recovery from the defaulting units. At the stage of sanction, sufficient care should be taken to see that only economically sound projects should be sanctioned credit. The collusion of the loanees and the staff of the Corporation have to be checked at this stage. The defaulting units should not only be debarred from getting future loans, but also they should be made ineligible for loans from any other financial institutions including banks.

IMBALANCE DISTRIBUTION

A large share of the financial assistance by the SFCs has gone only to a few districts. The imbalanced distribution of financial assistance is making poor districts poorer and rich districts richer. In case of APSFC, there is a wide variation in assistance provided to different districts or various zones. Especially the corporation had concentrated on the districts located near by the state capital only. It leads to further imbalanced regional development. It is essential to remove this regional imbalance. In order to develop the backward regions, more concessions should be provided to industries in the backward areas. A special fund should be created for providing assistance in these areas. The corporation should provide as much technical help as possible to industries established in backward regions. The SFCs should also assist units in facing their problems relating to production techniques, maintenance, accounting, taxation, procurement of raw-materials, marketing etc., The SFCs, apart from assisting the existing industrial units, have to identify the potential for establishment of new industries and should assist entrepreneurs willing to exploit the potential. For this, the district-wise survey of industrial and entrepreneurial potential will help the SFCs in increasing their business in backward areas.

MUCH DEPENDENCE ON IDBI

A major problem of the SFCs is that they have come to depend on the IDBI to a great extent. It is true, that the IDBI is an assured and also relatively cheap source of finance. As on 31st March 1996, the APSFCs borrowings from IDBI and RBI amounted to Rs. 375.22 crores accounting for 48.78 per cent in relation to total resource structure. It would be appropriate for the corporation to strengthen its internal sources by ploughing back the profits. It is possible only when the Corporation improve its efficiency by generating profits through effective management of funds.

Inexperience coupled with imperfect knowledge lead to increasing amount of arrears. Misuse of SFCs loans is yet another serious problem because of different interest rates charged on different categories of loans. Undue bureaucratic interference in the working of the SFCs also encourages the borrowing units to think that the loans are not necessarily repayable. These issues should be rectified and improve the performance of the APSFC in order to channelise its lending activities towards industrial development of Andhra Pradesh. This can be done with the committed efforts of the officials of the Corporation and the industrial entrepreneurs.

Financing of Business in North-Eastern Region--A Study of Assam Financial Corporation

Dr. (Mrs.) S.R. Borkotoky Sarmah *
Mrs. Ashima Sarma (Bora) **

In India, North East is one of the region which is densely populated and rich in natural resources. Capital formation is very low to provide stimulation for entrepreneurship development and to mobilise savings and investment, Assam Financial Corporation was established in 1954.

Now the corporation has to face the problem of shortage of working capital and hence main motive is also jeopardised. With the help of ratio analysis and other information, an attempt was made to prove the reality.

INTRODUCTION

NE Region is one of densely populated area with fertile alluvial soil in India. It consist of seven states as Assam, Meghalaya, Nagaland, Tripura, Manipur, Mizoram and Arunachal Pradesh. NER is rich in natural resource but its economic development is very slow. For economic development finance is the life blood. As it is a scarce resource it cannot be raised easily. With a view to promote and assist the capital scarce Government of Assam established Assam Financial Corporation (AFC) in 1954 under the SFC Act, 1951. AFC shares the pride of being a premier Financial Institution dedicated to the cause of industrial development in the NER. AFC was the second SFC covering its operational jurisdiction in the states of Assam, Tripura, Manipur and Meghalaya. The main objectives are to

* Senior Lecturer, Golaghat Commerce College, Assam.
** Lecturer, K.C. Das Commerce College, Guwahati, Assam.

provide loan assistance to SSI and MSI from 1954-55 and also limited working capital assistance also SSI from 1989-90 under single window scheme (SWS) in NER.

With this strong background we find that AFC has to face a very tough year since 1994-95. So, from their published informations regarding performance, recovery, Balance Sheet and Profit and Loss Account and share of Equity capital and borrowings. We want to find out the reality and its suggestions. For this purpose, we will use ratio analysis mainly (i) Funded debt to total capitalisation (ii) Debt to equity (iii) Equity to net fixed assets and (iv) Net fixed assets to funded debt.

We have choosen for these ratios as we are interested to study the working capital position of the AFC because its earnings decline day by day.

PERFORMANCE HIGHLIGHTS

With only nominal equity and borrowings infrastructure, the role of AFC in the industrial financing has been commendable. The state-wise sanction of loans during last 3 years together with percentage is given below :

TABLE—1
State wise sanction for last 3 years from 1994-95 to 1996-97

(Rs. in Lakhs)

	1994-95			1995-96			1996-97		
State	*No	Amount	%	No	Amount	%	No	Amount	%
Assam	93	515.07	88.0%	74	289.46	96.7	42	154.91	100
Tripura	5	36.43	6.2%	—	—	—	—	—	—
Manipur	4	24.07	4.1%	—	—	—	—	—	—
Meghalaya	1	10.00	1.7%	1	10.00	3.3	—	—	—
Total	103	585.57	100	75	299.46	100	42	154.91	100

Source : Annual Report 1996-97 of AFC p. 17.
* No of Application.

From the Table—1, it is clear that percentage of loan sanctioned for Assam is increasing but its total amount is decreasing.

For 1996-97, no application from outside Assam has taken for granted. Hence the entrepreneurs from outside or from assam is also deprived from getting loans.

The corporations paidup share capital has been comprised of (i) Contribution from various state Governments and IDBI. IDBI contributes nearly 47 per cent of total share (ii) Borrowings by way of refinance from IDBI and SIDBI Bonds and Deposits (iii) Recovery of loans etc. The following Table—2 indicates the composition of share capital as on 31st March '97.

TABLE—2

Position of Paidup Share Capital as on 31st March '97

(Rs. in Lakhs)

Particulars of Shareholders	Paid up Share Capital	Share Capital received in Adv.	Total	% age of Paidup Capital
Govt. of Assam	388.95	294.68	683.63	
Govt. of Tripura	40.45	20.00	60.45	6%
Govt. of Manipur	23.33	21.95	25.28	3%
IDBI	444.17	—	444.17	47%
LICI	9.60	—	9.60	1.5%
Scheduled Bank	14.15	—	14.15	2%
Cooperative Banks	2.00	—	2.00	.70%
Others	2.58	—	2.58	.80%
	925.23	316.63	1241.86	100%

Source : Annual Report of AFC 1996-97. p. 24.

(i) On the basis of the sources available as stated above in Table–2, the corporation has finalised the share capital contribution in the Annual Plan through Business Plan and Resource Forcast (BPRF) approved by the Small Industries Development Bank of India (SIDBI) and the Board of Directors as shown below:

1992-93	Rs.	105.00	lakhs
1993-94	Rs.	200.00	"
1994-95	Rs.	200.00	"
1995-96	Rs.	200.00	"
1996-97	Rs.	200.00	"
	Rs.	905.00	iakhs

Out of the above fixed share capital contribution from the participating state Govts. the corporation has not received any share capital from 1993-94 to 1996-97. The non-receipt of share capital contribution has resulted in severe gap in resource which has jeopardised the entire business plan of the corporation adversely.

TABLE—3
A Summary of Balance Sheet for last three years

(Rs. in Lakhs)

Particulars	As at 31.3.95	As at 31.3.96	As at 31.3.97
LIABILITIES			
Share capital	925.23	925.23	925.23
Share Money received in advance	316.63	316.63	316.63
Reserves	319.37	319.37	319.37
Bonds	4125.00	4780.00	5115.60
Other Borrowings	2183.70	1844.47	1779.47
Deposits	316.22	291.19	270.74
Subvention received from Govt. on account of dividend	35.33	35.33	35.33
Other liabilities	158.31	205.39	238.18
Provisions	126.91	3162.16	3321.16
Total =	8506.70	11880.37	12321.71
ASSETS			
Cash and Bank Balance	562.38	515.05	407.36
Investment	2.50	2.50	—
Loan and Advances	5654.33	6729.70	6773.06
Fixed Assets	157.90	136.96	126.57
Dividend Deficit Account	37.14	37.14	38.02
Other Assets	72.92	76.75	75.11
Advance Payment of Income Tax	190.88	190.88	190.91
Profit and Loss Account	1828.65	4191.39	4710.68
Total =	8506.70	11880.37	12321.71

Source : Annual Report 1996-97 of AFC p. 23.

(ii) The information from Balance Sheet shown in Table—3 for the last 3 years since 1994-95 to 1996-97 indicates that no additional share capital is contributed throughtout these three years, rather borrowed funds also diminishing from Rs. 2183.70 to Rs. 1779.47 in 1997. Borrowing is the second constituents of its capital.

From corporate information was can mention that " refinance loan from IDBI and SIDBI has been discouraged due to higher interest w.e.f. 1993-94. Further the IDBI has discontinued the matching share capital w..e.f. 1991-92."

(iii) The third constituents are recovery of loans etc. The BPRF generally fixed the recovery target. For 1996-97, the target was fixed at Rs. 1500 lakhs as against which the corporation recovered Rs. 632 lakhs which was 42 per cent of the targetted amount. Recovery achievement for the last 3 years are as follows :

Year	Amount
1994-95	Rs. 721.00 lakhs
1995-96	Rs. 691.00 lakhs
1996-97	Rs. 632.00 lakhs

The decreasing trend of recovery has a direct impact on its capital. A major portion of the operating capital i.e. 58 per cent or (632/1500 x 100) has blocked due to this reason.

RATIO ANALYSIS

Over and above those general observations if we analyse the Balance Sheet in detail with those aforesaid ratios we will find that :

1. The total capitalisation comprises long term debt capital and reserve. The ratio is computed and expressed as percentage. A too heavy debt burden reduces the margin of safety for lenders. A continuous inadequacy may invite insolvency and force reorganisation. For the last three years it goes up i.e. 80 per cent, 81 per cent and 82 per cent respectively.
2. To calculate Debt Equity ratio Debt includes only long term debt i.e., Rs. 6308, Rs. 6625.07 and Rs. 6895.07 respectively. Equity is fixed for three years is Rs. 1,561.23. Normally it should be 2:1. But in our case it is higher than 4 times. A higher proportion would be risky and it may effect the image of the corporation.
3. Equity to Fixed Assets given an indication of the extent to which equity capital is invested in net Fixed Assets. The higher the ratio means lesser the protection for creditors. For AFC it is also not satisfactory.
4. Fixed Assets to funded debt acts as a supplementary measure to determine the protection for the lenders. Standard should not be more

than 1. AFC's ratios are .025, .021 and .018 respectively. It means that long term funds are more than fixed assets and that funds are used for financing working capital.

Table—4 shows in details regarding the Ratio analysis.

TABLE—4
Ratio Analysis

	1994-95	1995-96	1996-97
Funded debt to Total Capitalisation	6308.70 / 7869.93 x 100	6625.07 / 8186.30 x 100	6895.07 / 5456.30 x 100
Debt to Equity	4.04 times	4.24 times	4.42 times
Equity to Net Fixed Assets	7.87 times	9.07 times	9.82 times
Net Fixed Assets to Funded Debt.	.025	.21	.018

OBSERVATIONS

(1) From the analysis of these statements we can conclude that the year 1996-97 as in the last three years also to be a tough year for the corporation particularly in the area of resource mobilisation for continuance of financial assistance to sustain concerted industrial development in the area of its jurisdiction.

(2) Recovery of loans did not pick up the projected level despite vigorous efforts due to various factors beyond the control of the corporation. All these factors compelled the corporation to curtail the sanction by adopting a cautious approach while considering new loan proposals.

(3) Diminishing trend of fixed assets may lead to the state of over capitalisation.

SUGGESTIONS

On the light of the above survey we suggest that:

(1) Norms for equity participations including Seven States should be modified and revised.

(2) Timely release of Prime Minister's Economic Package for NER may also help a lot in increasing share capital of AFC.

(3) Government should take bold steps towards protection of SSI and MSI units so that no. of sick units may reduced. Here bold step means Govt. may adopt some rating of agmark etc. for quality product so that in the competitive market they can stand independently.

In conclusion we should think for the revival of this corporation. So, all the wellwishers and corporation itself should come forward.

REFERENCES

Dhar. PK., '*A Text Book on Economics Vol. I*' published by Ashomi Prakashoni.

Hingorani Ramanathan Grewal., '*Management Accounting*.' Published by Sultan Chand and Sons New Delhi.

Kuchal S.C., '*Corporation Finance*' Published by Chitanya Publishing House, Allahabad.

Sherlaker S.A., '*Modern Business Organisation and Management*' Published by Himalayan Publishing House, New Delhi.

'*Annual Report: 1996-97*' Published by AFC.

New NBFC Policy—An Evaluation

Prof. J.V.Prabhakara Rao *
V. Surya Rao **

In the last 2-3 years there have been many developments in the non-banking financial sector. In the light of these, the Reserve Bank of India has recognized the need to introduce certain measures to curb the exaggerated business activities of this sector. This has led to the new policy of the Reserve Bank of India on non-banking financial companies putting an end to the NBFCs honeymoon with the policy of liberalisation in the financial sector. The present study focuses on various aspects of regulatory framework, recent developments in the NBFC industry, impact on NBFCs, relaxations in the new NBFC policy, change in impact due to the relaxations, missing links in the policy and is intended to recommend certain measures in tune with the NBFCs opinion to make the policy more feasible.

INTRODUCTION

The Reserve Bank of India recently announced guidelines on January 2, 1998, to regulate the functioning and working of NBFCs, particularly companies that accept public deposits to finance their businesses. Though the regulations are stringent and criticized as a knee-jerk reaction of RBI, such regulations are necessary to protect the interests of depositors. The action of the RBI was criticised as an over reaction to the CRB scam in 1997 given that it would be difficult for many NBFCs to immediately

* Senior Professor and Head, Department of Commerce and Management Studies, Andhra University, Visakhapatnam.

** UGC Junior Research Fellow, Department of Commerce and Management Studies, Andhra University, Visakhapatnam.

comply with the new regulations. Subsequently, on Jan. 30th 1998 the RBI relaxed those norms. We should welcome these regulations which will weed out the blade companies and protect the interests of investors. At the same time policy guidelines should be favourable for healthy companies to operate and contribute to economic development. Moreover, the new accounting guidelines under consideration will bring transparency and further strengthen the industry. NBFCs play a vital role in mobilising resources from the general public. They have the network even where banks do not have. NBFCs are extending credit to those sectors, which are not catered to by banks and financial institutions. Considering their contribution to the nation, they should be allowed to operate in the system freely with an optimum supervision and control by the regulatory authority.

WHAT ARE THE ACTIVITIES OF NBFCs AND WHO REGULATES THEM

Non-banking finance companies are those concerns rendering financial services similar to commercial banks and financial institutions, but do not qualify to be branded as banks. Hence their name goes as NBFCs. They accept deposits, they lend, they lease, and they operate mutual funds, and do a lot of similar functions. They are an integral part of the Indian financial system.

Most NBFCs are regulated by the Reserve Bank of India. The central bank prescribes the quantum of deposits these NBFCs can accept, the interest rate they should pay, etc.,

NBFCs are again classified according to the dominant activity undertaken by them. Thus, they can be loan companies, investment companies, hire purchase companies, leasing companies, nidhis, residuary non-banking finance companies (like Sahara and Peerless), depending on the classification, the regulatory framework vary.

INDISCRIMINATE GROWTH AND THE SHAKE OUT

NBFCs in India have been operating for quite a long time. They are large in number. From 7063 in 1981, it has risen to more than 45000 in 1998. Phenomenal growth, it is indeed. We may even put it as mushrooming. Yes, 21 per cent of NBFCs amount for 97 per cent total deposits, according to a RBI estimate. They have grown in a comparatively lose regulatory framework. Perhaps the growth has been due to absence of shackles. Taking advantage from the loose framework, some NBFCs like CRB, Sneham finance, Fair growth, Grow More, etc cheated the small depositors by closing their ventures.

RECENT DEVELOPMENTS

The latest scandal involving CRB appears to have generated considerable movement on the regulatory front. A whole set of conditions is being put into place; cash reserve ratio, statutory liquidity ratio, capital adequacy norms, exposure limits and audits by Chartered Accountants and the RBI. For the fault of a few black sheep the entire industry will suffer. Out of the 37000 applications received for registration, the RBI, it appears has shortlisted 8500 companies.

In the light of the recent developments in the non-banking finance companies sector, particularly in the last 2-3 years, the Reserve Bank of India, being the central administering agency, has acted swiftly in introducing certain measures purportedly to curb the exaggerated business activities of this industry.

Two important developments have taken place in the recent past in the field of Non-banking finance companies. The most important one was, of course, the amendment of Reserve Bank of India Act 1934. The amendment gives wide-ranging and sweeping powers to Reserve Bank of India. Second, RBI made major relaxation's in respect of the access to credit facilities as well as acceptance of deposits for those NBFCs which were registered with RBI, rated by rating agencies and observe prudential norms. Both these developments mark an important stage in the growth process of NBFCs.

In exercise of these powers, the RBI, by it's recent directions issued on January 2, has laid down fresh ground rules on the basis of which NBFCs will have to manage their activities in future. It is proposed to briefly discuss the salient features of the new regulatory framework of RBI on NBFCs and evaluate the policy framework from its desirability, practicability and other such related angles.

REGULATORY FRAMEWORK

The salient features of the new regulatory framework are as under:

1) For the purpose of the new regulations, NBFCs have been divided into three broad categories viz., those accepting public deposits, not accepting public deposits and NBFCs not accepting public deposits and have acquired securities in its group companies of not less than 90 per cent of their total assets.
While NBFCs accepting public deposits will be subjected to all the provisions, those, which do not accept public deposits, will be supervised in a limited manner.
2) Prohibition from accepting public deposits for NBFCs having net owned funds of less than Rs. 25 lakhs. For the rest, the ceiling on the quantum of public deposits has been linked to their credit rating.
3) NBFCs with AAA rating can raise three times their NOF through deposits if they are equipment leasing or HP companies and twice their NOF if they are loan and investment companies. For AA rated companies, the corresponding figures are twice and equal to their NOF respectively. Companies that are rated A can raise an amount equal to their NOF if they are equipment leasing or HP companies and half their NOF is they are loan and investment companies. NBFCs with a credit rating lower than A cannot accept public deposits. NBFCs that hold public deposits in excess of the prescribed limit will now have to refund them or otherwise regularise their position by December 31, 1998.
4) A 16 per cent ceiling has been fixed for interest on deposits.
5) Brokerage will be 2 per cent for all categories of deposits.
6) NBFCs that accept public deposits will have to file annual statutory returns and financial statements with the RBI. More important, all NBFCs that accept deposits will have to comply with a new set of prudential norms encompassing income recognition, accounting standards, asset classification, provisioning for bad and doubtful debts, capital adequacy and credit and investment concentration.
7) Capital adequacy has been raised form 8 per cent to 12 per cent, and is to be achieved in two phases by Mar. 31, 1999. Investment in a single company or a group of companies should not exceed 15 per cent and 25 per cent respectively of the NOF of NBFC concerned. NBFCs have also been advised not to grant loans against the Security of their own shares. Income recognition, asset classification and

provisionary norms of lease and hire purchase companies however, have been relaxed. Lease rentals that remain due for more than 12 months (against 6 months earlier) will now be classified as NPA. The liquid asset requirement will be the level of 12.5 per cent by April 1, 1998 and 15 per cent by April 1, 1999.

The apex bank has included a caveat emptor, cautioning deositors that a mere regulation cannot provide a fail-safe system of ensuring repayment of deposits.

NEW POLICY DIRECTIVES–IMPACT ON NBFCs

Measures	Impact
• Quantum of deposits linked to credit rating	NBFCs may have to return deposits Differential rating may create confusion
16 per cent Interest rate ceiling	NBFCs offering higher interest rates will have to roll back rates
• capital adequacy norms tightened	Reduction of risk on deposits
• Income recognition norms eased	Provisioning requirements to fall.
• Investment concentration norms tightened	Public deposits cannot be used to hold stakes of promoters.
• Liquid asset ratio changed	Maintenance of liquid assets to fall.
• Brokerage fees hiked	Additional incentives for brokers. garner more deposits.

The policy initiatives are in continuation of the regulatory initiatives, which were intensified after the CRB scam. Before analysing the changes, it would be interesting to look back on one important fact. Since one year or so… a difficult period for NBFCs, marked by adverse market conditions… the mainstream NBFC industry has always welcomed prudent regulations and has even suggested necessary regulatory and developmental measures to the RBI.

Today there is none among the responsible lot in the NBFCs who have any qualms over regulations, to the extent that they are prudent and are in appropriate dose. They would welcome regulation that is also developmental. The criticism, if any, therefore will be only about unnecessary tinkering, knee-jerk reactions and inconsistencies.

Linking the quantum of public deposits to rating of NBFCs look rational on the face of it but has its own problems. This will have a crushing impact on finance companies. Take the Managalore based firm ICDS, it was once considered as a top NBFC and had a triple A rating. Today that has been downgraded to A by the Crisil. Under the new rules, ICDS's fixed deposits are in excess of the ceiling by Rs. 323 crore and will have to be refunded when they fall due. Ceat financial will have to refund Rs. 482 crores. While complete data is required to determine those companies which may have to repay deposits, it is required to determine those companies which may have to repay deposits, it is not clear as to how companies can do so. In the absence of any alternative source of fund, it would mean forced liquidation of assets, and in some cases, the companies themselves. Already hit by the downgrading of credit ratings, reflecting the overall unfavorable industry scenario, the affected companies should find the going tough.

For most large NBFCs fixed deposits from the public has constituted the most important funding source. Sundaram Finance, which is the largest NBFC and has a triple A rating, raises 40 per cent of its funds from fixed deposits. Similarly, Lloyds Finance has deposits of over Rs. 500 crores. Companies like Sundaram, and even Kodak, Mahindra can still raise money and they have a long way to go before hitting the limit. But others like Lloyds, Mafatlal and Anagram have to first raise funds to repay the excess deposits.

As NBFCs will not be able to raise enough deposits, public deposits, public savings will get channeled into other areas. Bank deposit rates are already low and the present decision will also dampen interest rates further. There could be a tendency to consume rather than save and savings growth rate could also see a dip. NBFCs play a significant role in the countries financial system and also assume higher risks than commercial banks, extending loans for trucks, tractors, commercial vehicles, cars and consumer durable. These are the areas where banks do not readily extend financing and where they do so procedures are so elaborate and rigid that consumers shy away from approaching them. While severely restricting the route of accepting fixed deposits, RBI has not opened any alternate avenues of raising resources by NBFCs NBFCs can only finance India's vast rural and semi-urban markets.

The relaxation with regard to classification of lease and hire purchase assets as NPAs from the earlier stipulation of 6 months past due to the revised 12 months past due is definitely welcome. Considering the present scenario of industrial slowdown, defaults and the recovery experience of the entire financial system. This clearly shows that the RBI has kept in mind the collections and recovery scenario, while fixing NBFC norms.

The increase in minimum capital adequacy will also create pressure and restrict the number of NBFCs accessing public deposits. Consolidation and mergers are likely to follow soon. Though the RBI has no legal powers to force mergers, on an informal basis it may play a matchmaker role.

RELAXATIONS IN THE NEW NBFC POLICY—A BREATHER

Jan. 2nd, 1998	**Jan. 30th, 1998**
Leasing COs rated below A cannot accept public deposits	COs with minimum investment grade (A–, BBB, BBB-) can accept deposits
NBFCs have to regularize excess deposits by Dec. 31st, 1998	Time frame extended to Dec. 31st, 2000
Unrated COs cannot mobilise public deposits at all	Unrated COs can renew maturing deposits
Preference shares not included in NOF	NOF to include Preference Shares

Within a month of having slammed on NBFCs by imposing a stringent set of regulations, RBI loosened its regulations even before NBFCs made any efforts to comply with them.

The RBI, in its new circular, has extended the time limit for regularisation of the excess deposits to Dec. 31st, 2000. As per the new directives, the minimum investment grade refers to companies, which are rated FA—by Crisil and ICRA, BBB by CARE and BBB-by DPI. In addition to this the limits for these companies have also been enhanced. Equipment leasing and hire purchase finance companies which carry a AAA rating can raise public deposits upto 4 times their NOFs now against three times earlier, while AA rated companies can raise now upto 2.5 times and A rated firms upto 1.5 times their NOF, while the minimum investment grade companies can mobilise public deposits equal to 0.5 times their NOF.

CHANGE IN IMPACT-MIXED BAG

It seems, RBI has accepted 80 per cent of the industry's demands. The move allowing less than A grade companies to raise funds to the extent of 0.5 tines their NOF could see roughly 300 more companies joining in the line. The relaxations announced by RBI can be described as 'Positive And Pragmatic'. Now there would be no pressure on any NBFCs to set their houses in order by regularising the excess deposits collected is reality based. While enhancing the limits for fixed deposit collections is appreciated. I do not think any triple A rated company really needs to collect deposits, 3 or 4 times their NOFs. It is not clear—why unrated companies have been allowed to renew their deposits.

Though the series of relaxation measures announced by RBI for NBFCs has come as a big relief for the leading players in the industry, smaller firms with lower rated and those unrated cannot be happy. With rating made mandatory, big names in the industry like Shri Ram group, Shakti Finance, MCC Finance, besides several small players are barred from accepting fresh deposits.

DIRECTIVES—NOT YET IN FULL MEASURE

RBI has failed to stipulate what action would be taken against those who default in payment of fixed deposits, who fail to meet the criteria or exceed the prescribed limits. And another surprising thing is that, fixed deposits accepted by manufacturing companies have not been touched bay the fresh set of regulations. As a result, the objective with which RBI initiated new regulations is not clear. Is it just to reduce the number of NBFCs in the country? Rather the objective should have been to discipline the companies accepting fixed deposits and initiate strict punitive measures against those defaulting in repayments and those exceeding the prescribed limits.

PRESCRIPTION FOR NBFC ILLS—MISSING LINKS

1) Only listed companies should be allowed to invite public deposits.
2) Deposit holders should be treated on par with shareholders and sent all the relevant information, including annual reports.
3) Ban on incentive payment to depositors.
4) The effective interest rate should be disclosed.

5) The unsecured nature of the instrument could be a constraint from the safety point of view. There is no insurance coverage for NBFC deposits. Government should build a deposit insurance scheme at a nominal premium of 0.005 per cent p.a. The premium rate should only provide for administrative costs to run the scheme. If there are losses to be met, then ad-hoc demands for additional premium could be made.
6) There is no tax incentive for investors who invest their money in fixed deposits—there is a TDS if the income from interest is above Rs. 2500 per annum. Absence of congenial tax climate may be a handicap while promoting the scheme.
7) State Governments should have a role to play in regularising the activities of NBFCs, as this would supplement the efforts of RBI and Central Government in controlling NBFC activities.

In the light of the above, it is clear that the latest regulatory framework —which indeed is very stringent–is a reaction to the CRB type fiasco. What should have been done is more naunced and, to that extent, shifting NBFCs from an unduly loose framework to a suddenly tightened one is clearly a knee-jerk reaction of RBI. What might have been done is that the practicality should have been kept in mind initially. In that way the stakeholders' world have bot been put to any great, or sudden, hardship or losses. Prescription of low is not enough better administration of law that is what needed from RBI.

Probably the best part is when the RBI says "Whatever be the rigorous of regulation, the regulations by themselves cannot provide a fail-safe system for ensuring repayment of deposits". In fact, the RBI has a lot more than depositor protection to do. Development of all segments of the financial system, including NBFCs, should also be on its agenda.

Today, there is none among the responsible lot in the NBFCs who have any qualms over regulations, to the extent they are prudent and are in the appropriate dose. They would welcome regulation that is also developmental. The criticism, if any, therefore will be only about unnecessary tinkering, knee-jerk reactions and inconsistencies. It is in this context that the latest changes seem to be a mixed bag. Whatever may be the impact on industry and reaction of people, this move is welcome. There should be some discipline in the industry otherwise, the depositors will be affected.

REFERENCES

Dr. A. C. Shaw, 1997, '*Finance Companies'—Agenda for Urgent Action*' (Mumbai: Forum of Free Enterprises).

Abhijit Roy, 1997, '*Whither non-banking finance companies*', The Hindu—Business Review, Dec' 17.

Mahesh Thakkar, Ramu S Deora and J.D. Agarwal, 1998, '*Cap on NBFC: Stringent But Late?*', The Economic Times, Page 7, Jan. 13.

'*Investor's guide on finance companies, 1998*', Integrated Enterprises Limited.

NBFCs—The Tragedy of Economic History of Modern India

Dr. K.S. Vataliya *
Mr. H.D. Vyas **

INTRODUCTION

Many countries tested fruits of Liberalisation, Privatisation and Globalisation (LPG) and people of these countries are also getting their share according to contribution. While some countries experienced adverse results of the same. And because of these results, economic existence of those countries has become endangered.

Since 1991 Indian authorities opened the door for LPG. As a part of this LPG process, many relaxation were declared in numerous areas of economy and production. As per that financial sector was also deregulated to such extent for private Indian and foreign companies. Due to this many national and Multinational companies activated their activities in the area of Banking and Non Banking financial services too.

Currently Indian economy is passing through the situation of liquidity. Because beginning of LPG attracted many newcomers in financial market. They also began their activities in many areas of financial sector. But inefficiency of some of them put their existence in dangerous situation, which affected their investor's economics too. So jungle law of survival is prevalent in Indian financial market at present.

We aspire to study the above in this paper. The objectives of this paper is defined as (I) To study current position of Non Banking Financial

* Senior Lecturer, M.J. College of Commerce.
** Lecturer, M.J. College of Commerce, Bhavnagar University, Bhavnagar.

Companies under Highlights (NBFCs), (II) Present scenario, (III) Survival of fittest, (IV) Lessons from experience and (V) Conclusion.

HIGHLIGHTS

1. Many companies, which are providing financial services to private sectors have disappeared or they have been at last stage of end.
2. There is great disappointment and atmosphere of mistrust in this field. And the investors have lost crores of rupees.
3. In India, the atmosphere is like law of seas were big fish swallows smaller, as per that huge and giant NBFC Companies or foreign companies are swallowing smaller NBFCs.
4. In past, large number of banking companies and financial institutions dreamed to expand their activities all over the world, but now only 10-12 players aim to expand their activities at world level.
5. Compared to India, large and Multinational NBFCs in Britain, Germany, France and Japan feel wisdom to work in specific product and in particular field geographical area.
6. In India NBFCs are providing only financial services particularly lending activity. A very few NBFCs use skills or specific knowledge in the fields.

PRESENT SCENARIO

The situations like last stage of world war in the field of financial services are prevailing in India. Before five years, all Industrial Houses were eager to tap in this field and so many COs were incorporated in financial services. They created euphoria in Indian capital market and as a result they issued their shares with high premium in the open market, and Indian investors were also ready to get the share at very high price without considering any norms of logical investments. During these period, a number of companies have offered their issues in the market to gain investors' sentiment and collect millions of rupees from public. Public has lost crores of rupees due to failure of familiar and unfamiliar financial companies during last 5 to 7 years in our city. Number of companies have disappeared and remaining is at the last stage of TB. A very few companies have survived, Industry scene is like a battlefield, where numbers of dead bodies are lying, others are handicapped and a very few soldiers are saved. This is the present seen of NBFCs of private sector.

As per experts' opinion such situation is due to keen competition in some fields, Norms for securities are neglected or not considered due to eagerness for enhancing business and overall bad conditions of the industry. Last layer of faith of investor is shacked by recent issue of CRB. As a result, possibilities of gaining money from public on competitive base are decreased and reached at last stage. In such a situation, it is difficulat for Indian companies to start in market against more aggressive Banking companies, Government and Semi Government financial institution specifically huge foreign financing companies.

SURVIVAL OF FITTEST

Karl Marx says in his book 'Dascapital' that if capitalisation is to be spread freely in the world, and restriction should not been forced on it any where in the world, then 50 to 100 companies will be established their economic power in near future all over the world. Today when geographical boundary and artificial walls are going to break and consequent economic transaction are also going to more free, then it seemed that world is going to the path of forecasting of Karl Marx.

GE. capital, Morgan Stanley and Goodman Soch are going to cover Indian market strongly. In the initial stage, these international Cos. fail in the Indian Market but it is cleared they will be succeed in long run as their basis are strong and huge for setting up the high losses. As fish law, "big fishes are swallow smaller fish'. J.E. capital swelled 1 or 2 Indian Cos. up to this date, ICICI swelled ITC classic finance and now it is ready to absorb Anagram Finance Via merger. Now other many Indian financial companies are in line to be a foods of such giant companies. Now the days are not far away that financial service sector will remain for big players. Smaller Cos. are going to be disappeared. City Bank, A.B.N. Amro and United Bank of Switzerland are gradually increasing their presence at world level. Even though they learned through experience that it is not wise to offer each product to each market in every country.

As for Spokesman of Mecknzey and Company of NewYork, "Before some decades, there were about 50 countries in battles to lead the world in the field, which gradually decreased and reached at the No.of 20 Cos and at present only 10-12 Cos. are in line.

Infect few financial Cos. or banks are expanding their activities with such ambitions. Many banks and financial institutions want to work in particular market with specific product instead of expanding their activities around the world.

LESSONS FROM EXPERIENCE

Such multinational NBFCs has to pass through many kinds of experience, (good and bad) and change their future strategy. It is universally going to accept that the true power of the company is its product on which the construction is most important. The company who wants to go abroad has to consider local culture of concern country. According to Prof. Ghoreli, of international business school of Losan, the companies who wants to expand their activities have considered enough about its financial strength and skills, technology, strategy etc. but they are failed due to avoiding cope with local culture. [Such type of Cos. have to create belongings in the company by employing more and more internal experienced men from various countries.] There are about 9000 high level managers in City bank are non- American and in its branches, out of them several are famous in their activities in the country.

At last, it is important that you develop your name as brand name around the globe, then success will be in your hand.

CONCLUSION

Thus, particularly in India and around the world, there is quite disorder in the capital and money market. We learned a lesson in India after experience of huge losses. In the last decade, leasing and financial cos. which grew like string warm in India research work has been done except lending the money neglecting security aspect. Our forefather were also lending money and today we get money under the 'English' words, collecting money from public, it is not new and it will not change the Universal principals and rules. Even though having high means, companies did not use specialised skills and knowledge in a specific field. They did not contribute anything except huge expenses. A large Nos. of Indian NBFCs are just like a tragedy of economic history of modern India.

Corporate Ethics —A Dilemma between Economic and Social Performance

Dr. Omprakash Kajipet *

In today's corporate world, the issue of 'ethics' is being talked of on many occassions due to several reasons. The terms, and that question,—what is 'right' and 'proper' and 'just', in corporate management in general and in management of private and multinational corporations in particular, are going to be more important than ever. They are going to be critical in the future than in the past as our *society becomes more crowded*, our *economy* more *market -oriented and competitive*, our *technology more complex*, and our *attitudes more materialistic.* These terms are particularly more important for the corporate managers, whose decisions can affect so many people in ways that are outside their control. Thus, corporate ethics is an issue of contemporary relevance and it continues to be a matter of greater attention of the policy makers, managers, social scientists and also the Government in the years to come.

More often than not, the terms, 'corporate ethics', 'business ethics', and 'management ethics' are used interchangeably. In essence, they refer to the philosophic doctrine of management of a corporate enterprise, signifying observance of moral principles, a code, and a normative or value system in serving the society and the nation at large, besides meeting the corporate's economic objectives.

CORPORATE ETHICS AND CORPORATE GOVERNANCE

Corporate governance, in usual sense, refers to the accountability—relationship between the board of directors (managers) of a company and

* Reader in Department of Commerce and Business Management, Kakatiya University (Satavahana Post-graduate College), Karimnagar - 505 001 (A.P.).

its shareholders (owners). Corporate governance relates to building the institutional framework for business operations and deciding the boundaries within which these functions would be performed. The essence of good governance is to achieve the right balance between shareholders and management interests. Good corporate governance and corporate performance go hand in hand. However, Good corporate governance and corporate ethics do not necessarily mean the same. Corporate ethics, essentially sets the philosophy and provides a direction in building an appropriate organisational system and culture, which forms the most important element in corporate governance. Corporate ethics and governance are closely inter-linked and one complements the other. Corporate ethics thus, covers a broader spectrum of interests and people than the corporate governance.

Corporate ethics emphasizes the practice of high *ethical standards, ensuring proper values, higher degree of transparency* and especially *accountability,* not only to the shareholders and also to the society and nation. It also involves the *balancing of interests of various groups*— employees, customers, suppliers, distributors, members of the society or public, and shareholders with which a corporate body usually deals with. It often goes far beyond the simple questions of bribery, theft, and collusion. It focuses on serving the every section and segment of the society/nation in an effective manner apart from satisfying the economic interests of the owners and management of a corporate body.

ISSUES IN CORPORATE ETHICS

The most critical issue in the corporate ethics is the *resolution of the continual conflict between the economic performance of the corporate bodies,* which is often measured in *terms of revenues, costs, and profits and owned to the shareholders* or to their owners and the social performance of such bodies, measured in terms of *their responsibilities and obligations* to the *society/nation in general, members of the general public, customers, suppliers, employees, creditors in particular.* Another contentious issue in corporate ethics is how *to measure or judge the social performance of corporate bodies in precise terms so as to evaluate it against their economic performance.* Thus *the resolution of continual conflict between economic and social performance is not an easy task and it gives rise to ethical dilemmas on many occassions in corporate* management.

Ethical dilemmas in corporate management are not easy choices between 'right' and 'wrong' and, they require and do involve a careful and thorough analysis of various economic, legal, social and moral forces, and complex judgements on the balance between economic returns and social damages, complicated by the multiple alternatives, extended consequences, uncertain probabilities, and career implications that are inherent part of these decisions.

The complexity of decisions on ethical dilemmas in corporate management can often be stated simply and directly that:

1. *They have extended and far-reaching consequences.* The affect and influence of such managerial decisions and actions do not stop at the corporate-level and have an impact beyond the corporate levels, i.e., on other groups of the society.
2. *They have multiple alternatives/choices.* It is often presumed that the ethical issues in management are primarily dichotomous, a yes, and no choice, but no other alternatives. But there will be multiple alternatives in making ethical choices.
3. *They have mixed outcomes.* Social benefits and costs as well as financial revenues and expenses are associated with almost all of the alternatives in ethical choices.
4. *They have uncertain consequences.* Often, the manager was not clear and certain about the consequences that follow from the alternatives considered in most of the ethical choices.
5. *They have personal implications.* It is commonly thought that the ethical issues in management are largely impersonal, divorced from the lives and careers of the managers. But most of the alternatives in ethical decisions have an impact on financial and social benefits and costs and on individual benefits and costs as well.

The ethical dilemmas between economic and social performance in corporate management may often be the result of:

— pricing of products and services at a particular level
— designing of advertising messages and contents of truth
— promotion of products and services in a particular fashion
— provision of after-sales customer-service with conditions

— reduction of work-force
— ignoring environmental pollution on emission of industrial wastes
— relations with suppliers, community, social, religious, and other organisations and agencies.

The crucial question in resolution of ethical dilemmas, i.e., decisions and actions faced by corporate managers in which the economic performance and the social performance of the corporate bodies is in conflict, is how to decide, how to find a balance between the two. The balance between economic and social performance is very much necessary to ensure and maintain corporate ethics in managerial decision making process.

In a competitive world, it is always not possible to take decisions in situations of ethical dilemmas in favour of social performance. At the same time, it is also not possible to ignore the social performance completely in favour of economic performance, while making decisions in such situations. Therefore, the crucial question in corporate ethics is where to draw a line between economic and social performance of an organisation and how to balance them or to find a trade-off between them.

It is often stated that there are three forms of analysis that can help in drawing the line, that can assist in reaching a decision on the proper balance between economic and social performance. These forms of analysis are economic, based upon impersonal market forces; legal, based upon impersonal social forces; and philosophical, based upon personal principles and values. Since, the canvass of this paper is confined to crucial issues in corporate ethics, no attempt is made to examine the forms of analysis mentioned above in detail. However, it is to be remembered that none of them is completely satisfactory in resolution of ethical conflicts between economic and social performance of an organisation. Sometimes, it may be useful to attempt all the forms of analysis together to arrive at a decision in situations of ethical dilemmas.

CORPORATE ETHICS IN INDIAN CONTEXT

The debate on corporate ethics and good corporate governance is getting hotted up in recent times on account of several reasons. These may include—increased pressures from more discerning and objective shareholders on companies for better economic and social performance, significant presence of foreign institutional investors, changed role of nominee directors from banks and financial institutions on corporate boards. More importantly, the detection of several incidents of misgovernance, manipulation, and inadequate commercial and social accountability appears to be the principal reason responsible for growing attention and emphasis on corporate ethics and quality corporate governance in the country. For instance, many corporate bodies in the recent years have resorted to unlawful activities and violation of various business laws mainly to boost up or show better economic performance to its shareholders. A list of such companies is furnished in Exhibit—1.

Of the cases furnished in Exhibit—1, the cases of ITC and Shaw Wallace companies really made every one alert and careful about corporate ethics and good corporate governance in corporate circles. Now everybody is seriously thinking about the good corporate governance and ethics. Strictly speaking, none of these cases really involved an ethical dilemma, and they do simply depict misgovernance and manipulation. But the ongoing Tata Tea episode, which is in the news now-a-days, throws open many issues of corporate ethics in Indian corporate circles. The details of the case are given under.

CASE OF TATA TEA LIMITED

The Tata Tea Limited in August, 1997, has assisted Ms. Pranati Deka, the Cultural Secretary of ULFA, a militant outfit of Assam, in her medical treatment at Mumbai, by spending nearly about Rs. 75,000 to Rs. 1,00,000 under the Specialised Medical Assistance Schemes (SMAS) of the Company.

In this context, the Assam State Government alleged that there is a prima facie case against the Tata Tea limited under Section 10 of the Unlawful Activities (Prevention) Act, as they have assisted the operations of the ULFA through contributions and also in other ways. It also pointed out the involvement of the top officials of the Company in funding the ULFA militants in Assam and also personal contacts between senior executives with ULFA Chief. All this clearly amounts to "conspiracy against the State" according to the Government.

On the other hand, the Tatas have sought to shelter themselves against the State Government's charge of having links with secessionists by the retort that it is the failure of the authorities to provide security to the tea companies that forced them to humour the militants. The company also came out with a statement that there are sanctions from Intelligence Bureau for alleged Tata-ULFA meetings in India and abroad, and the Assam Government was kept abreast of all the demands that the ULFA has raised on the Company periodically. They argue that the payments of protection money to the militant outfits was the result of failure of the Central and State Governments to tackle the insurgency problem and near-collapse of security. Further, the Company pleads that it has never made cash payments to the militants except that it has assisted the member of the ULFA under the existing SMAS as a part of its programme of Community Welfare and Social Welfare and Development. There were forced meetings between the Company and ULFA in India and abroad in the interest of safety of its officials, since, one of its managers was already shot dead, another was kidnapped and held in captivity for 11 months, and two were kidnapped and held for 48 hours.

The Government, however, criticised the arguments of the Tata Tea, providing medical treatment to the members of militant outfits was clearly an aberration from the SMAS, and the correspondence and meetings with the outlawed outfit clandestinely, clearly amounts to acting against the interests of the State. The Government also came out with a statement that there are intelligence reports that both private and public sector companies are paying protection money to extortionists belonging to insurgent groups. The government outrightly dismisses the industry's alibi of helplessness saying, "the corporates could not violate laws and ethics by siding with terrorists, whey they knew that security was a State responsibility".

The respective positions taken by the Tata Tea Limited and the Assam Government in the matter of decision to assist a member of the ULFA and alleged involvement of senior officials of Tata Tea in funding the ULFA militants are shown in Exhibits—2 and 3.

In this case of Tata Tea Limited, the crucial question is, whether the company's decision to assist the members of ULFA in medical treatment under its welfare schemes, to maintain the personal contacts and hold meetings with militant outfits in the interests of safety and security of its officials, is 'right', 'proper', and 'just' or not. It is beyond doubt that whatever has been done by the Company in the circumstances narrated, is to protect its own business interests and economic returns. But the Government dismisses its stand and points out that it is a clear violation of laws and ethics, and its actions amount to anti-national and conspiracy against the State. The judgement in this matter is not an easy choice of between 'right' or 'wrong' and requires a careful analysis of economic, legal, social and moral forces involved in the entire episode.

CORPORATE ETHICS AND ETHICAL CODES

A more desirable approach in resolving ethical dilemmas is *formulation of ethical codes of conduct with a certain degree of professionalism. Ethical codes are statements of the norms and beliefs of a corporate enterprise.* These norms and beliefs are generally developed by a team of senior executives in the organisation, which explain the *standards of behaviour in situations of ethical dilemmas—conflicts between economic and social performance.* Ethical codes also express a general sense of the *obligations of members of corporate bodies feel towards the different groups such as employees, customers, suppliers, distributors, and the general public or society at large.*

Another approach to sustain high ethical standards and thereby ensuring proper values is, *to design systems and procedures with a greater degree of transparency in corporate dealings with several groups and greater accountability to different groups and the society.* Therefore, the need of the hour is to emphasize on every corporate body to evolve a code of conduct keeping in view the ethical values and its strict observance for quality corporate governance through managerial ethics in the years to come.

EXHIBIT—1

Company	Violation
ITC	Fera
Shaw Wallace	Fera and I-T
Voltas	Excise Duty
Kirloskar Pneum	same
Blue Star	same
Alfa Laval	same
Premier Auto Ltd	Fake Bookings
DCM Daewoo	Sales Tax
Nestle	Customs and Fera
HDC	Income Tax
Ganapati Exports	Customs

Source : Economic Times, January 1, 1997.

EXHIBIT—2

TATA TEA LIMITED

Tata Tea categorically refutes allegations of any involvement in anti-national activities

It is a fundamental obligation of every State to protect the lives and property of its citizens and also provide security to industry in the State. In the past one decade, the State of Assam has neither been able to fulfill this obligation nor control the militant organisations holding the State and its industries to ransom.

As a result, over the years, several attempts have been made to terrorise Tata Tea and its officials by millitant organisations in order to extort money. The attempts have been made through threatening phone calls to, and forced meeting with, company officials.

At all such forced meetings in India and abroad Tata Tea, even at risk to the safety of its officials and their families, refused to meet the militants' demands in cash or kind. This is despite the fact that one of the Company's managers was shot dead, another senior manager was kidnapped and held in captivity for 11 months, and two other managers were kidnapped and held for 48 hours before being rescued.

As a part of its policy to undertake charitable and welfare activities, Tata Tea has plainly told the millitant organisations that it would undertake welfare activities in the State of Assam and for the Assamese people but would neither generate nor pay any money. The above activities of the Company and meeting held have been undertaken with the knowledge of the authorities concerned. The Company has contemporaneous documentary evidence to prove this.

The welfare activities undertaken include the construction of hospitals, vocational training centres, lab to land programmes, out-reach medical camps and also the provision of specialised medical treatment outside Assam. These schemes are available to all. The treatment of a lady patient alleged to be linked to ULFA at Mumbai was under the specialised medical treatment scheme mentioned above.

A copy of a letter dated 4/1/96 from Tata Tea to ULFA has been selectively released to the press mischievously highlighting just one portion of the same. Even in this letter, the Company has plainly refused to pay any money to ULFA, while re-affirming its commitment of undertaking welfare schemes only. Prior to issuing this letter, the Company had met the then Home Secretary of Assam and had sought the State's protection and assistance to deal with this threat. Unfortunately, no effective assistance or help was provided. Thereafter a copy of the Company's letter of 4/1/96 addressed to ULFA was sent to the State Government under a covering letter dated 9/1/96. The Government of Assam has therefore been fully aware of this letter and also the Company's stand for the past one year and nine months. It is therefore surprising that after such a lapse of time this letter has now surfaced in the press and is being used to discredit and tarnish the image of the Company.

Tata Tea is extremely proud of its integrity and its people, who have worked in Assam at great personal risk to themselves and their families. The Company has never acted directly or indirectly in any illegal manner and its actions have been transparent in keeping with its long-standing traditions.

Issued by Tata Tea Limited.

EXHIBIT–3

ASSAM GOVT. FLAYS TATA TEA OVER 'CONTRADICTORY' ADS

Our Special correspondent
Guwahati 22 September

The Assam government on Monday criticised the advertisement campaign launched by the Tata Tea in some of the national papers which according to the state government is quite contrary to the stand of Mr Ratan Tata, chairman of Tata Sons.

Senior government officials stated that Tata Tea, in their advertisement issued on Monday, has stated that Ms Pranati Deka, Cultural Secretary of ULFA was treated under their Specialised Medical Assistance Scheme (SMAS) while Mr Ratan Tata had admitted in New Delhi that the treatment of Pranati Deka " was an aberration from the SMAS".

They feel providing 'A' class comforts in posh hotels and hospital of Bombay to Pranati Deka and her escorts, who are themselves hard-core ULFA activists, and beinge scorted by a senior executive of Tata Tea. Dr. Brojen Gogoi is outside the scope of their much talked SMAS. The State government on Monday issued a press release where they have mentioned that the state government is well aware of their constitutional duties and during the last sixteen months of their being in power not once have the officials of Tata Tea complained about security threats to Tata Tea or its employees working in Assam.

The release states that through the advertisement Tata Tea has admitted that they have been meeting with militant organisations abroad. They said it can not be understood how Tata Tea or for that matter any other Indian tea company can forced by the ULFA or NDFB to meet outside India, "unless there is some element of tacit understanding leading to the organisation of such meetings abroad. The state government also takes note of the fact that Tata Tea has not kept the state government informed about such clandestine meetings abroad with persons/ organisations who are waging war against the country."

It states that it was only at the initiative of the State Chief Minister, Mr P. K. Mahanta, that a meeting with the CCPA was held in Guwahati on 13 November 1996 to discuss the problems faced by the tea industry in the State.

Corporate Ethics —Some Influencing Factors

Prof. K. Rajeshwar Rao *
Dr. P. Krishnama Chary **

It is very difficult to define the term, 'ethics' precisely, since it covers a multitude of business decisions, practices and policies. One must be careful in generalising about it. Perhaps the best criterion for judging how important ethics is to person is, how much he scarified in terms of position, money, time and energy in order to act ethically. Ethics refers to the code of conduct and moral duty and concerns human relations with respect to right and wrong. Ethics also concerns morals and philosophy. Ethical rules differ from legal rules in as much as the former are not enforced by public authority, whereas the latter are. Legal rules become unnecessary when ethical rules are observed by businessmen. Society expects the businessmen to act ethically.

Ethics implies the study of the morality of human actions; it is regarded that 'being ethical' means acting according to reason and that 'unethical' action can be shown to be unreasonable. It is helpful to bear in mind the distinction between i) what one knows or believes to be ethical, i.e., his standards, ideals, or code, and ii) what one does i.e., his actions. There is often a disparity between one's standards and his behaviour usually the former are higher.

More often than not the businessmen argue that the businessmen is no different from anybody else. He must observe the same principles everybody else does, no more and no less. But this is merely to say that

* Members on Faculty, Department of Commerce and Business Management, Kakatiya University, Warangal - 506 009 (A.P)

the businessman, like every human being, must do good and avoid evil, and that certain general ethical norms are applicable to business activities.

There are certain actions, however, which are the unique of special concern of business, and the specific problems and opportunities confronting the businessman differ from those faced by others, for example, the politician, or the physician. As a consequence of these differences, questions arise about applications of ethical principles. This is especially true when a new economic situation arises, or when two or more principles seem to apply to a specific case. For example in deciding whether or not to move a plant from one city to another a business problem, several principles must be considered, and they seem to be in conflict; private property and the rights of stockholders are involved, as are the company's obligations to loyal employees and to the local community.

There are, then actions of businessmen in business situations, which are not found in other areas of life. The study of the object, intention, circumstances, and outcome of these actions of their rightness or wrongness, is the domain of business ethics.

RELEVANCE OF CORPORATE ETHICS

Ethics in corporate management assumes relevance in the context of the following. Ethics is not only important in the private life of individuals but also in the business affairs of a corporate body, where its decisions may affect the lives of thousands of its employees, customers, and members of the general public. Moreover, the most people want to be part of an organisation, which they can respect and be publicly proud of, because they perceive its purpose and activities to be honest and beneficial to the society.

A corporate body perceived by the public to be ethically and socially responsive will be honoured and respected even by those who have no intimate knowledge of its actual working. There will be an instinctive prejudice in favour of its products. Since, people believe that the company offers value for their money. Its public issues will attract an immediate response.

Another point of great importance is that an ethical attitude helps management to make better decisions, i.e., decisions, which are in the interest of the public, their employees, and the company's own long-term good, even though decision making is slower. This is so because respect for ethics will force a management to take various aspects, economic, social, and ethical aspects into consideration. In the long-run ethics and profits go together. A company which is inspired by ethical conduct is also profitable one. Value driven companies are sure to be successful in the long run, though in the short run they may lose money.

Ethics is important because government law and lawyers cannot do everything to protect the society. People in an industry often know the dangers in a particular technology better than the regulatory agencies. Further, the Government cannot always regulate all activities which are harmful to the society. Where law fails, there ethics can succeed. An ethical oriented management takes measures to prevent pollution and protect workers' health even before being mandated by the law.

CRITICAL ISSUES IN CORPORATE ETHICS

Corporate ethics essentially involves ethical dilemmas between right and wrong or desirable and undesirable, which emerge out of different decision making situations. Some of the situations of ethical dilemmas, being encountered by the corporate managers are presented hereunder.

In designing of advertising messages for the products developed by the Research and Development wing of a corporate body, which are not really new and improved, the corporate manager will be in a dilemma to state the same or not knowing that the sales will only improve, if it is stated otherwise in the message.

In decisions concerning the recruitment of key functional executives, who worked with the competitors and capable of revealing the strategies of the competitors, the manager may be faced with a dilemma, whether it is ethically right to recruit them or not.

Similarly, in situations of getting new accounts in an attempt to improve sales, through a bribe or gifts to the purchasing agents, often the managers encounter an ethical dilemma whether to resort to such actions or not.

In situations of products, or services having an established relationship between their use and adverse effects on the health and safety of its consumers like drugs, liquor, cigarettes etc., the product managers may have to face the ethical conflict as to whether to sell or not.

In circumstances of loop-holes in the existing tax laws one may be facing a dilemma as to whether it is ethically 'right' to exploit such loop-holes to reduce the tax burden instead of making use of the tax incentives provided in the tax system.

In all the situations narrated above, the ethical dilemmas can be resolved by the means suggested by phillip kotler. According to him, all ethical philosophies deal with one or more of three characteristics of the act. They judge the act itself (moral idealism), the actor's motives (institutionism) or the act's consequences (utilitarianism).

a) Moral idealism is the most rigid and postulates certain acts to be had in all or most circumstances. Moral idealism gives managers a definite answer in the above cases. For example, the manager would not print the statement in the message, and he would not hire the manager and so on, by refusing to let the end justify the means. Managers, would have a stronger feeling of correct conduct.
b) Institutionism is less rigid, leaving it to the individual managers to sense the moral gravity of the situations. If managers feel that their motives are good and that they do not intend to hurt anyone they proceed with the decision making. They are taking an intuitive approach to morally difficult situations.
c) Utilitarianism seeks to establish the moral locus not on the act of the motives but on the consequences. If the consequences represents a net increase in society happiness or at least not a net decrease, the act is right.

INFLUENCING FACTORS

The experience teachers that good ethics is good business. It implies four ideas pertaining to customer or employee relations, in the following order of importance.

1. Customers and repeat sales.
2. Employees, union and low turnover.
3. Good reputation.

4. Consistent behaviour.

A moment's reflection on the four ideas reveals how reasonable it is that a customer who is treated well may return to the same store or salesman; that employees like to work for a manager who respects them; that most men are pleased to do business with a company that has a good reputation; that consistent behaviour is valued by manufacturers and retailers. In other words, experience teachers that ethical behaviour and good business practice often coincide.

The businessman exists for only one purpose; to create and deliver value satisfactions at a profit to himself. If what is offered can be sold at a profit, then it is legitimate. The spiritual and moral consequences of the businessman's actions are none of his concern. Most of the corporate executives affirm that : "for Corporation Executives to act in the interest of shareholders alone, and not also in the interest of employees and consumers, is unethical". Further, the aim of the corporation should not be profit maximisation but rather a performance of excellence".

Although we know little about the acquisition of moral knowledge and attitudes, it is clear that they depend in large measure on the advice and example of the adults with whom a person spends his childhood. These acquiring of moral knowledge continues throughout the life, for example, through one's wife, boss, or peers.

It is evident from the experience that the persons with the most beneficient influence on the decisions of these businessmen are those who dealt with them when they were young. This suggests that, for ethical business decisions, attitude may be more important than knowledge. By attitude we mean a conviction that is important to act ethically and a desire to do so.

Awareness about ethical problems and the ability to think and speak about them is improved by college, especially if it includes a course on ethics. But there is no evidence that decision making is more ethical as a result of college course. Businessmen want the schools to produce recruits who will not harm the image of their company by unethical decisions and many businessmen favour college courses in business ethics.

The most important influence on an industry's ethical practices is competition, both the amount and the kind. Competition is related to factors like elasticity of demand, homogenity of product, ease of entry into the industry, and the rate of growth of demand for the product. It is to be noted that beyond a certain point (call it the ethical optimum of competition), as competition increases, so do the unethical practices.

It is suggested that a kind of moral Darwinism prevails in corporate world, with the less ethical companies dying in the long run. This may be true in industries in which product quality can be identified by the average purchaser, or in which frequent repeat sales are the pattern.

It is also observed that the moral equivalent of Gresham's Law is operative, with unethical business practices driving the ethical ones out of the market place. This is another way of saying that the lowest common denominator behaviour tends to prevail in a highly competitive situation. This view down grades the influence of the professional managers and well intentioned executives who make key decisions.

The challenge which made businessmen to improve the upward trends in tnterest, knowledge, and behaviour with respect to business ethics. One of the major obstacles to this improvement is a selfish and unethical minority of businessmen. This group exercises a bad influence, which is disproprotionate to the number of men involved. The reason is, once again, competition. Although a few businesses operate in a perfectly competitive market, many businessmen react to unethical competition as though their only option were to duplicate their opponent's every action. Their assumption seems to be that the best way to fight economic fire is with fire. Not encough businessmen are willing to take a reduced profit rather than lower themselves to the ethical levels of competitors. Perhaps one reason is that few customers are willing to pay extra for ethical behaviour by the seller unless it is accompanied by economic advantages.

APPROACHES TO CORPORATE ETHICS

One way of making business ethical is to enact legislations and enforcing them rigidly. This will discipline the errant businessmen. But laws are no substitute for ethics. As was stated above, law cannot protect the society always.

The ideal way is to make businessmen frame their own Codes of conduct and adhere to them. The process of drawing a Code and its adherence should be institutionalised. Such institutionalisation would involve three steps.

1. Drawing up a Company policy or Code of ethics.
2. Familiarising all employees with the Code.
3. Ensuring the implementation of the Code by means of a formally designated 'Ethics Committee' of the Board of Directors.

In the present climate of business, the material needs of millions in this country are satisfied only through behaviour that is usually ethical. Achieving a higher level of business behaviour will require the habitual practice of justice and charity by the businessmen. By reading and reflection, they must upgrade their knowledge of business ethics. By financing research, they must deepen what is known about this complex field. Improvement will require co-operation among businessmen and representatives of the other sectors of the community. But basically, though improvement can be aided and hastened by external means like voluntary Codes of ethics and governmental agencies, business behaviour must be improved from within man by man. A businessman is a man before he is a manager, and the more ethical, reasonable, and human he is, the better man-manager he will be.

Corporate Governance in India — Retrospect and Prospects

T. Bharath *
Dr. Omprakash Kajipet **

Corporate governance is essentially the philosophy by which companies are to be directed and controlled. Corporate governance, in its usual sense, refers to the accountability—relationship between the Board of Directors (Managers) of a company and its stake-holders. Boards of Directors are responsible for the governance of their companies. With the separation of ownership from management, the primary responsibility for running the business of a company with integrity lies with the managers, who are accountable to all the stake-holders, particularly to the owners for their stewardship function. The responsibilities of the Board include setting the company's strategic aims, providing the leadership to put them into effect, supervising the management of the business and reporting to the shareholders on their stewardship. The Board's actions are subject to laws, regulations and the shareholders in the annual general meetings.

Corporate governance can therefore, be defined as a system of structuring, operating and controlling a company with specific aims of fulfilling the long-term strategic goals of the owners; consider and care for the interests of employees, past, present and future; take account of the needs of the environment and the local community; maintain excellent relations with both customers and suppliers; maintain proper compliance with all the applicable legal and regulatory requirements.

* Members on the Faculty, Department of Business Management, Satavahana Post-graduate College, Kakatiya University, Karimnagar-505 001 (A.P.)

PRESENT SCENARIO

In the context of globalisation of our economy there is a concern at every quarter of economic system that the corporate governance in India should conform to international norms. The levels of transparency and standards of disclosure observed by the Indian corporate sector at present is far from desired levels. The practice of placing personal interests above those of other stakeholders is quite widespread. Although public listed companies have 'outside' Directors on the Board of Directors, this is often for the sake of formality and image rather than substance. Even in respect of Boards on which institutional lenders and investors have appointed nominees, there is no genuine independent and external scrutiny of executive managers.

The failure in ensuring good corporate governance in India is due to a variety of factors. A few of such factors are discussed hereunder.

First, the excessive regulation of the economy through rigid controls, a lot of bureaucratic discretion in decision-making, and political interference in the process—constitute one set of factors.

Another set constitute—limited market competition through industrial and import controls and resultant neglect of cost, quality and competition in a shortage economy. The end result was corruption, granting favours for consideration and overall erosion of value system. Unsatisfactory business ethics has to be seen as part of this environment.

Second, there was neither regulatory nor market pressure for good corporate governance. For good performance neither efficiency nor quality were necessary. Despite pervasive controls, and comprehensive supervision from various 'watch dogs' such as government departments, lenders, institutional nominees on the Boards, in reality the managers had their own way in running businesses. This can be attributed to two reasons. One, financial institutions condoned many shortcomings of corporate management and were permissive and tolerant because they perceived their developmental role as promoting import substitution industries. Secondly, some financial intermediaries either out of carelessness or incompetence, failed in protecting their interests with vigilance. The lack of sufficient autonomy also contributed to the failure. Wilfull connivance and complacity, either at the behest of the politicians and bureaucrats or for personal gains, struck a major blow to corporate governance.

Finally, the so called professional managers and independent auditors did not contribute much in ensuring good corporate governance in India. Many of them became willing or unwilling partners in poor corporate governance. The main focus was on performance, which was narrowly defined. So long as operations remained profitable, lenders, principal investors, auditors and Boards did not look at finer aspects of performance such as the quality of earnings and soundness of accounting practices. Even problems surfaced, corrective actions could not be taken promptly because neither the judicial system nor the agencies like the BIFR has succeeded in dealing expeditiously and effectively with recalcitrant and incompetent management. Even secured lenders have been struggling to exercise their security in several cases for over 10 years.

As a consequence of the above, corporate governance today is intensively debated upon amongst the leaders of business, bureaucrats and the heads of the financial institutions. The recent interest about corporate governance is primarily a product of four factors.

1. The more awareness and assertion of rights by the shareholders.
2. The significant presence of Foreign Institutional Investors (FIIs) who are demanding greater professionalism in the management of Indian corporates.
3. There is a greater awareness on the part of lending institutions in recent times, which are now being subjected to rigorous accounting norms, particularly with regard to income recognition and provisions against non-performing loans. So they are giving much more emphasis to good and efficient corporate governance.
4. The integration of Indian economy with global economy which demands that Indian industry should play the game by a standard set of international rules rather than continue their anachronistic practices.

Because of the above factors and also with economic liberalisation, pressure on managers to improve the quality of corporate governance is mounting. We have witnessed a sea change in the economic environment during last few years. Good number of shackles have been removed and considerable operational freedom is now available to the management. As a result, the overall corporate scene has become quite dynamic and lively. There is a virtual scramble among the corporates to increase turnover, improve profitability and boost up the earning per share. Obviously, to attain these objectives, a good number of restructuring and re-engineering exercises are taking place. Lot of discussion and deliberations are held in corporate conclaves on what business one should be in, what business one should retain and from what business one should get out. The buzz word is healthy and ever improving bottom line. Never before, the Indian corporates have applied their minds more seriously to the above game plan. Vision development exercise and the follow-up retreats are a common phenomenon. In this backdrop coroporate governance acquired importance for sustainable development and survival of companies.

ISSUES IN CORPORATE GOVERNANCE

One of the key-traps to avoid in thinking about corporate governance is the mistaken view that it is simply the system whereby a company controls its risks. This view leads to a rather negative approach, instead of looking for a system that stimulates entrepreneurial drive whilst balancing it with a framework of control.

Another trap is to tackle the topic by developing a series of piece-meal proposals, which are struck onto the existing legal framework, instead of developing a holistic view of the proper framework for good corporate governance.

The basic governance issues relate to the effectiveness and the accountability of the Board of Directors. Effectiveness is measured by performance. How well do Boards run their companies and how can they be encouraged to run them better? Effectiveness is therefore, a measure of the quality of the leadership provided by the Boards in directing and managing their companies and the test of effectiveness is the results those companies achieve.

Accountability is largely a matter of disclosure. transparency of explaining a company's activities to those to whom the company has responsibilities. Accountability raises the question of to whom are companies answerable? and to whom should they be? One of the reasons why corporate governance is on the international agenda is that there is a demand from institutions of all kinds to account publicly for their decisions and actions. Board of Directors are seen as having power and relative freedom to exercise that power with in the law. The demand for Boards to become more accountable is therefore, a part of a wider movement for openness by institutions.

ROLE OF BOARDS IN CORPORATE GOVERNANCE

The Companies Act, 1956 provides the formal legal framework for corporate governance in India, wherein the Boards of Directors are given crucial role to play. The effectiveness of a Board depends on the ability of the Directors, who make it up and the way in which they work together. The Indian company law contemplates unitary Board system and the division of the Board into two categories of Directors, executive and non-executive. The spirit of company law clearly is that the Board should function as a unitary body and act collectively so that the collective wisdom of the Directors is pooled for the benefit of the company. All the Directors are equally responsible in law for the Boards' actions and decisions.

The Board of Directors is the supreme governing organ of a company. This is evident from the Section 291 of the Companies Act. 1956, which states that "subject to the provisions of this Act, the Board of Directors of a company shall be entitled to exercise all such powers, and to do all such acts and things, as the company is authorised to exercise and do". This supremacy is subject to two limitations, namely, first that the Board shall not do anything which is required to be done by the shareholders and second anything done by the Board should be in accordance with the provisions of the law, memorandum and articles of the company. Thus, the Board is the custodian of the interests of the company and stakeholders.

The structure of Indian Boards traditionally is such that in many cases they are dominated by Directors coming from or having loyalty to either promoters of the company or a family or group of persons having controlling interest in the company. This dominance is displayed in two ways. First, these Directors are in majority on the Board. Secondly, the positions of Chairman and Executive Directors are filled from amongst these Directors .The role of non-executive Directors, who are some times called ornamental or status Directors has hither to been not very significant.

ROLE OF FINANCIAL INSTITUTIONS (FIs) AND INSTITUTIONAL INVESTORS

Over a period of time, financial institutions have made an entry into corporate Boards through financial participation and assistance. They have also brought some measure of discipline and objectivity in the decision making process of the corporates. Rightly FIs have supported existing managements, as loans are sanctioned based on the track record of promoters running the business and the repayment of loans depended on the ability of the promoters to run the business successfully. This would also ensure a fair return on their investments in the company. While this is in the self-interest of FIs, the larger interest of the corporation seems to have taken a back seat. However, in recent years the role of FIs have come in for severe criticism because of their passive role so far. Their nominee Directors, who are mostly their own employees, have not been able to act independently in the decision making process. They are not to be blamed as they have not been told of the larger vision in the corporate management or have they received any kind of specialised training in this regard.

Today, India has a matrix of shareholding, where the dominant players are financial institutions, the public on an average is the second highest holder of equity in companies, the third and forth are promoters and the foreign institutional investors (FIIs) respectively. We usually have a situation, where most of the companies in India are controlled by promoters with an average shareholding of 8 to 12 per cent. Until recently the financial institutions were passive investors and lenders. Since, the major financial institutions have now started to increasingly rely on stock and debt markets for funds, they are forced to adopt a more active management style to protect their interests on behalf of their own investors.

ROLE OF SHAREHOLDERS IN CORPORATE GOVERNANCE

The shareholders' role in governance is to appoint the Directors and the auditors and to satisfy themselves that an appropriate governance structure is in place. The formal relationship between the shareholders and the Board of Directors is that the shareholders elect the Directors and the

Directors report on their stewardship tc the shareholders. The shareholders appoint the auditors to provide an external check on the Directors financial statements. Thus, the shareholders as owners of the company elect the Directors to run the business on their behalf and hold them accountable for its progress and performance. The issue of corporate governance before shareholders therefore is, how to strengthen the accountability of Directors to shareholders.

While an individual shareholder is ineffective, he can definitely make an impressive mark as a member of the shareholder group. For the same reason, the Indian Companies Act envisages meetings of shareholders for various purposes. However, they have not been able to perform their due role effectively for the reason that they are widely spread and many of them find extremely difficult to travel to the meeting place. The spread of equity cult, which resulted in virtual explosion of shareholder's group has further worsened the situation. The capital market reforms initiated by SEBI have not been able to bring any substantial improvement in the matter of shareholders role in corporate governance.

ROLE OF THE STATE IN CORPORATE GOVERNANCE

The legal and procedural aspect impinging on the quality of corporate governance are set by the statutes enacted by Parliament. These are—Companies Act, MRTP Act., FERA, Consumer Protection laws, Capital Market Regulations. Depositories Act, Arbitration and Conciliation Act etc. These legislations set the minimum level of governance by the corporates. Those who have achieved the minimum level of governance are better poised to achieve better governance and the ultimate goal should be to achieve better than the best and a cut above the rest.

The minimum level of governance is not a static concept, but keeps changing on in tune with the changing economic environment and social ethos. The new economic policy of 1991 and the subsequent trade related reforms in the area of industrial licensing, monopoly laws, capital market reforms, changes in import and export policies, foreign exchange regulation etc., have set new norms, for better corporate governance. There is an increasing emphasis on self-regulation on the part of corporates and the State intervention has been reduced to the barest minimum. This is a reflection of the confidence, which the State has reposed in the corporates in their ability to manage their affairs in the larger interest of our economy and of those who are directly or indirectly concerned with corporate governance. This casts a larger responsibility on the corporates and this has to be reflected in the better corporate governance.

PROSPECTS FOR GOOD CORPORATE GOVERNANCE IN INDIA

With the separation of ownership from the management, the primary responsibility of running a business of a corporate enterprise with integrity and efficiency lies with the managers (usually the Board of Directors) , who are accountable to the owners (i.e., the shareholders) for their stewardship function. It is a well accepted theory that the only way to improve the corporate governance in India is to maximise 'contestability'. Contestability refers to a competitive pressure in an apparently incompetitive arrangement.

A corporate governance system aims to build contestability within the organization. The underlying principles of an ideal corporate governance system are:

1. It should be effective in protecting shareholders interests, yet should leave managers free to run and develop business and should take risks and show entrepreneurship;
2. It should provide transparency in terms of full disclosure of information to enable shareholders to evaluate managers in their stewardship functions and to be decisive if managers are not performing as per expectations;
3. It should not adversely affect investors liquidity and must allow shareholders to buy and sell shares freely;
4. It should not encourage insider-trading; and
5. It should not impair the competitiveness of the organisation.

The prospects for the corporate governance in India depend on a hoist of steps and some of these are presented hereunder.

The effectiveness of a Board depends on the ability of the Directors who make it up and the way in which they work together. First, the non-executive Directors should be selected through a formal process and that this process should involve the Board as a whole, which will reinforce the independence of non-executive Directors and make it evident that they have been appointed on merit and not through any form of patronage. A formal selection process should start with a review of the existing Board to identify the gaps in the Board in terms of experience, personality, age and skills. A purposeful search can then be put in hand to identify individuals who would fill these gaps and add value to the Board. The company's aim has to be to form the best Board it can, not just an acceptable Board. They should be appointed for a specific term and reappointment should be on the basis of performance but not as routine.

Non-executive Directors should bring an independent judgement to bear on the issues of strategy, performance, resources, including appointments and standards of conduct.

It is highly desirable that, all the Directors, both executive and non-executive should undergo some kind of training before or after their induction into the Board.

The fee to non-executive directors should reflect the time which they devote to the companies affairs and the value of the contribution made by them.

The Chairman's role in securing good corporate governance is crucial. It is for the Chairmen to make certain that their non-executive Directors receive timely, relevant information tailored to their needs. Given the importance and particular nature of the chairman's role, it should in principle be separated from that of the chief executive. If the two roles are combined in one person, it represents a considerable concentration of power hence, they need to be separated one from the other to ensure good corporate governance.

In many companies world over including a few in India, non-executive Directors as members of aduit committee, are providing constructive services in improving the quality of corporate governance. Membership of the audit committee should be confined to the independent non-executive Directors. It should be formally constituted so as to ensure that they have a clear relationship with the Boards to whom they are answerable and to whom they should report regularly. They should be given written terms of reference. The effectiveness of an audit committee depends on the competence, commitment, and independence of its members as also on its terms of reference, access to information and availability of resources.

The executive Directors' pay should be subject to the recommendations of the remuneration committee, made up of wholly of non-executive Directors. There should be full and clear disclosure of Directors total emoluments. Separate figures should be given for salary and performance related elements and the basis on which the peformance is measured should be explained.

It should be the Board's duty to present a balanced and understandable assessment of the company's position to all the stake-holders from time to time. The Directors should also report on the effectiveness of the company's system of internal control. Further, they should report that the business is a going concern, with supporting assumptions or qualifications as necessary.

For all listed companies the quality and quantity of disclosure that accompanies a GDR issue should be a norm for any domestic issue. It is further needed that the auditors should be changed atleast every three years to ensure better corporate governance.

REFERENCES

Ashish K. Bhattacharya (1996) "*Corporate Governance*". The Chartered Accountant. pp. 14-22, Volume XLV No 5.

Sir Adrian Cadbury (1997), "*Developments in Corporate Governance*", Chartered Secretary, pp. 487-490. Vol. XXVII No. 5

MacDonald Nigel (1997), "*Corporate Governance*". Chartered Secretary, pp.491-494 Vol. XXVII No. 5.

Jhoweri N.J. (1997), "*Corporate Governance : Why and How ?*", Chartered Secretary, pp. 495-496 Vol. XXVII No. 5.

Shaw R. Chinubhai (1997), "*Corporate Governance : Critical Issues,*" Chartered Secretary, pp. 497-500 Vol. XXVII No. 5.

Rao Prahlada D.K. (1997), "*Corporate Governance : Multifaceted Issues,*" Chartered Secretary, pp. 501-504 Vol. XXVII No.5.

Chandratre K.R. (1997), "*Role of Board of Directors in Emerging Dimensions of Corporate Governance and Impending Changes in Company Law*", Chartered Secretary, pp. 505-511 Vol. XXVII No. 5.

Athreya M.B. (1997), "*Are Ethics Irrelevant in Business*", Chartered Secretary, pp. 511-514 Vol. XXVII No. 5.

Srivastava R.L. (1997), "*Role of Directors Nominated by Financial Institutions*", Chartered Secretary, pp. 515-515 Vol. XXVII No. 5.

Mathur S. B. (1997) "*Corporate Governance : Concept and issues*", Chartered Secretary, pp. 516-519 Vol. XXVII No. 5

Mehta D.S. (1997), "*Corporate Governance : Role of Professionals*" Chartered Secretary, pp. 520-523 Vol. XXVII No. 5.

Mitra Amit (1997), "*Corporate Governance : A Transnational Phenomenon*", Chartered Secretary, pp. 524-526 Vol. XXVII No. 5.

Bebber D.K. (1997), "*Board Dynamics in Indian Public Enterprises*" Chartered Secretary, pp. 527-530 Vol. XXVII No. 5.

Narang S.P. (1997), "*Development of Corporate Governance in India*", Chartered Secretary, pp. 531-537 Vol. XXVII No. 5.

Varadarajan D. (1997) "*Corporate Governance and Legislative Reforms*", Chartered Secretary, pp. 538-541 Vol. XXVII No. 5.

Report of the *Company Affairs Committee of the Confederation of British Industry.*

The Report of the *Working Group on Redrafting of the Indian Companies Act.*

Proceedings of Seminar on "*Role of Nominee Directors, Financial Institutions : Obligations and Functions*" held on 27 and 28 January 1975 at Bombay.

Bansal C.L. (1989), "*Boardroom Practices in India—A Study*".

Railly Ray "*Globalising Management*", Published by John Willy and Sons.

Report of the Cadbury Committee on Financial Aspects of Corporate Governance, 1992.

Draft Report on Corporate Governance " Desirable Corporate Governance : A code" by the Confederation of Indian industry published in Business Standard 23-04-1997.

Ramaiya.A (1995), "*Guide to the Companies Act*", Wadhwa Sales Corporation, Dhantoli, Nagpur - 440012.